THE APPARENT
MEANINGLESSNESS OF LIFE

Abdellatif Elhomani
The Apparent Meaninglessness of Life

Published by Spines
ISBN 979-8-89950-502-7

THE APPARENT MEANINGLESSNESS OF LIFE

ABDELLATIF ELHOMANI

This book is dedicated to my lovely grandmother, Khadijah Alkhadri, and my sweet little daughter, Maryam Khadijah Elhomani.

CONTENTS

ABOUT THE AUTHOR

Dr. Abdellatif Elhomani is a distinguished engineer and researcher with a profound background in both engineering science and philosophy. He is currently serving as a Senior Principal Engineer at Northrop Grumman's F-35 Program. His career has spanned a diverse range of roles and industries, including positions as a Senior Mechanical/Reliability Engineer at Altec Industries and a Research Associate at Washington University School of Medicine.

Dr. Elhomani's academic journey is equally impressive. He earned a PhD in Engineering Science, a Master of Science in Manufacturing Systems, and a Master of Science in Mathematics, all from Southern Illinois University, Carbondale. His scholarly work, including his dissertation on "Thermal Models of Mechanical Systems with Frictions," highlights his analytical and interdisciplinary approach. His expertise extends into published research on topics ranging from thermal modeling to statistical analysis, demonstrating his commitment to advancing both theoretical and practical aspects of engineering.

In addition to his technical prowess, Dr. Elhomani has a keen interest in existential philosophy. This interest is vividly reflected in his book, The meaninglessness of life. Inspired by Albert Camus's concept of the universe's "benign indifference," the book challenges traditional views of meaning and purpose by integrating philosophical inquiry with scientific insights. Dr. Elhomani's ability to intertwine the existential philosophies of Camus, Schopenhauer, and Nietzsche with evolutionary theories by Darwin and Dawkins offers a unique and thought-provoking perspective on life's inherent absurdity.

Dr. Elhomani's diverse background and rigorous analytical skills make him well suited to explore profound questions about existence and meaning. His work invites readers to engage deeply with the complexities of the human condition, offering a framework for understanding personal significance in a seemingly indifferent universe.

ACKNOWLEDGMENTS

Writing The meaninglessness of life has been a journey of profound exploration and personal growth. I am deeply grateful to those who have supported and guided me throughout this process.

First and foremost, I must express my heartfelt appreciation to my wife, Madina Ikramova. Her unwavering support, patience, and encouragement have been the cornerstone of this endeavor. Her insights and understanding have provided me with the strength to persevere through the challenges of writing and researching, and her belief in my work has been a constant source of inspiration.

I also want to extend my gratitude to my colleagues and mentors who have influenced my thinking and contributed to my understanding of both existential philosophy and scientific inquiry. Their intellectual guidance and constructive feedback have been invaluable in shaping the content of this book.

Additionally, I am grateful to the institutions and organizations that provided the resources and environment necessary for my research. Their support has enabled me to delve deeply into the complex issues discussed in this book.

To my readers, thank you for embarking on this philosophical journey with me. I hope that the insights shared in these pages will spark meaningful reflections and discussions.

Lastly, I acknowledge the countless hours of dedication and effort that went into the writing of this book. This work stands as a testament to the collaborative spirit and support that made it possible.

With sincere thanks,

Abdellatif Elhomani.

PREFACE

In an age where questions of purpose and significance are as prevalent as ever, The meaninglessness of life embarks on a profound exploration into existential analysis. At its core, this book challenges the conventional notions of meaning and value by examining the universe through a lens of apparent indifference.

This book is hugely inspired by Albert Camus's concept of the universe's "benign indifference." With each chapter, we'll delve deeper into the notion that life, at its most fundamental level, lacks intrinsic purpose. Camus's idea suggests that the cosmos is indifferent to human concerns and aspirations–a perspective that will serve as the foundation of our examination. However, this exploration is not merely philosophical. It will extend into the realm of empirical science, engaging with the insights of evolutionary biologists like Charles Darwin and Richard Dawkins.

The meaninglessness of life weaves together the philosophical musings of Camus with those of Arthur Schopenhauer and Friedrich Nietzsche. Schopenhauer's profound pessimism about the human condition and Nietzsche's radical rethinking of values and the concept of the Übermensch ("Overman" or "Superman") will offer critical perspectives on the search for meaning in this book. Meanwhile, Darwin's and Dawkins' evolutionary theories will add the much-needed scientific backdrop that challenges traditional views of purpose and existence.

By synthesizing philosophical wisdom and scientific inquiry, this book aims to provide a framework for understanding the multifaceted nature of existence and offer insights into finding personal significance in a universe devoid of intrinsic purpose. The primary objective here is to foster a deep engagement with the complexities of the human condition and the quest for personal meaning. Rather than entering into debates or polemics, The meaninglessness of life invites you, my dear reader, to grapple with the intrinsic absurdity of existence.

It is important to clarify that this book is not an endorsement of atheism, nor is it written from an atheistic standpoint. While it critically engages with themes often associated with secular philosophy, the intention is purely exploratory and philosophical. The discussions herein aim to illuminate various perspectives on meaning and existence—not to promote disbelief in the divine or to negate the spiritual dimensions of life. The author respects all beliefs and approaches this subject with the hope that readers, regardless of their worldview, will find value in reflecting on these profound questions.

PART ONE
PHILOSOPHICAL
FOUNDATIONS

CHAPTER 1
THE ABSURD AND THE
SEARCH FOR MEANING

1. DEFINITION OF THE ABSURD

THE CONCEPT OF "THE ABSURD" pinpoints the fundamental conflict between humanity's desperate quest for meaning and the universe's apparent indifference toward it. This is central to existentialist thought, particularly in Albert Camus's works, where it presents a profound existential dilemma:

Conflict Between Desire and Indifference: The absurd arises from the paradox between the intrinsic need of humans for a purpose and the disregard shown by the universe. Naturally, humans seek coherence, understanding, and meaning in their lives, driving philosophical inquiry, ethical reasoning, and personal ambition. However, the universe does not care for it because it operates according to its own principles, which are indifferent to human concerns and lack intrinsic purpose or purpose (Camus, The Myth of Sisyphus, 1942).

Here's a real-life example: a high-level corporate executive who has dedicated decades to career success achieves significant wealth and status but still feels a profound sense of emptiness. Despite all the accomplishments, the universe remains indifferent, and that success does not necessarily bring deeper existential satisfaction to that person.

Now, how can absurdism be distinguished from existentialism?

Recognition of Absurdity: The absurd becomes apparent when individuals recognize the gap between their search for meaning and the universe's indifference. This awareness reveals that, despite relentless pursuit, the universe does not offer the answers they seek (Nagel, The Absurd, 1971).

Consider the same executive from the previous section as an example of this concept. This person eventually understands that their career success does not provide the ultimate fulfillment they anticipated. Realizing that their achievements are inconsequential in the grand scheme of things exemplifies the recognition of absurdity.

Existential Realization: This recognition often leads to existential frustration and challenges to belief systems and values. The absurd serves as a lens to examine the conflict between human purpose and cosmic meaninglessness (Sartre, Being and Nothingness, 1943).

Continuing with the example of the corporate executive, let's say that upon recognizing the apparent meaninglessness of their career, the executive experiences disorientation and questions the values that motivate their ambitions. This reflects the existential realization of the absurd.

2. CAMUS'S PHILOSOPHY OF THE ABSURD AND ITS IMPLICATIONS FOR HUMAN EXISTENCE

Albert Camus's exploration of the absurd, particularly in The Myth of Sisyphus, offers a nuanced understanding of the existential conflict and its implications. Let's take a closer look:

Camus's Concept of the Absurd: Camus argues that the absurd emerges from the clash between the human desire for clarity and the chaotic, indifferent universe. He says that, inherently without meaning, life defies attempts to impose purpose, leading to existential revolt, where one acknowledges absurdity without succumbing to nihilism (Camus, The Myth of Sisyphus, 1942).

For example, a successful tech entrepreneur may achieve significant financial success but find themselves questioning the ultimate purpose of their accomplishments. This confrontation with the absurd— recognizing that their success lacks intrinsic purpose— illustrates Camus's concept.

The Myth of Sisyphus: Camus uses Sisyphus, the tyrant king from Greek mythology, who was condemned by the gods to eternally roll a boulder up a hill only for it to roll back down, as a metaphor for the human condition. Despite the futility, Sisyphus as a symbol of absurdity of his task. This metaphor illustrates finding personal fulfillment despite an indifferent universe (Camus, The Myth of Sisyphus, 1942).

Let's return to the tech entrepreneur. Rather than viewing their work as a means to an ultimate end, they might come to see it as a continuous source of personal meaning. By embracing the absurdity of their circumstances and finding satisfaction in the process itself, they can experience a sense of fulfillment—much like Sisyphus, who discovers joy in his eternal struggle.

Implications for Human Existence: Camus boldly suggests that, rather than succumbing to despair or clinging to false illusions of meaning, individuals should confront the absurd directly and cultivate personal meaning through engagement with life's experiences and relationships. He further asserts that embracing this condition allows for passionate and authentic living, even in the face of life's inherent meaninglessness (Camus, The Plague, 1947).

An example of this would be the tech entrepreneur shifting their focus to enjoying present moments, building meaningful relationships, and pursuing personal passions. This approach embodies Camus's call to live passionately and authentically despite recognizing the lack of intrinsic purpose.

3. TENSION BETWEEN HUMAN DESIRE FOR MEANING AND THE INDIFFERENT UNIVERSE

Existential philosophy has explored this tension as a central theme in various ways. Some of these are:

Human Desire for Meaning: Humans are driven by a need to understand their existence and find purpose through philosophical inquiry, religious faith, artistic expression, and personal ambition. This search for meaning often involves imposing structure and significance on life through values and goals (Kierkegaard, Fear and Trembling, 1843).

For example, a talented musician dedicates their life to creating art, driven by the hope that their work will provide personal satisfaction and contribute meaningfully to the world. This pursuit reflects the human drive to find purpose through creative expression.

The Indifferent Universe: The universe operates according to natural laws and cosmic processes that do not accommodate human concerns or offer intrinsic purpose or moral guidance. Scientific discoveries highlight the vastness and randomness of the universe while emphasizing its indifference (Darwin, On the Origin of Species, 1859; Dawkins, The Selfish Gene, 1976).

For example, a scientist studying the origins of the universe may uncover the complexity and scale of cosmic processes, only to realize that the universe remains indifferent to human values and aspirations. This underscores the absence of an overarching purpose in the natural world.

Existential Tension: The stark difference between the human quest for meaning and the universe's indifference can lead to existential angst and disillusionment. The realization that human aspirations may be met with the universe's indifference can prompt an identity crisis (Taylor, Sources of the Self, 1989).

For example, an individual who has achieved career milestones may experience a crisis upon realizing that their life feels devoid of deeper meaning despite their accomplishments. This sense of disillusionment reflects existential tension.

Responses to the Tension: Philosophical responses to this tension include embracing the absurd (Camus), creating personal meaning through individual actions (Sartre), and finding solace in personal and communal connections (Frankl, Man's Search for Meaning, 1946). Each response addresses the challenge of the clash between human desire and the universe's indifference.

For example, after experiencing existential tension, a person might create their own purpose through personal projects and relationships, reflecting Sartre's notion of existentialism. Alternatively, they may find solace in meaningful connections or personal values, just as Frankl promotes by stressing the importance of finding meaning through suffering and responsibility.

To summarize what we've discussed so far, absurdism encapsulates the fundamental conflict between humanity's search for meaning and the universe's indifference. Camus's philosophy provides a framework for navigating this conflict and emphasizes the importance of embracing the absurd and finding personal fulfillment despite the apparent lack of intrinsic purpose.

CHAPTER 2
NIETZSCHE'S NIHILISM
AND THE ÜBERMENSCH

1. FRIEDRICH NIETZSCHE'S CRITIQUE OF TRADITIONAL VALUES

FRIEDRICH NIETZSCHE (1844-1900) is famous for his radical critique of traditional values and established systems of thought. His work challenges the very foundation of Western morality, religion, and metaphysics, proposing a revolutionary rethinking of human values and perspectives.

Critique of Christian Morality: Nietzsche's critique of traditional values is closely tied to his rejection of Christian morality. He argued that values such as humility, meekness, and self-denial stem from what he called "slave morality"—a moral framework born out of resentment by the weak toward the strong. In contrast to the "master morality" of the noble and powerful, slave morality inverts values, glorifying suffering, weakness, and subservience. Nietzsche contended that Christian morality suppresses human vitality and creative potential, fostering a culture of dependency, guilt, and passivity (Nietzsche, On the Genealogy of Morals, 1887).

In contrast, "master morality" celebrates qualities such as strength, pride, and assertiveness, viewing them as expressions of life's vitality and excellence.

Revaluation of Values: Nietzsche called for a "revaluation of all values," advocating for a fundamental reassessment of the ethical and moral principles that have long guided human behavior. He challenged the established norms and values of his time, arguing that they were artificial constructs created to suppress individual creativity, strength, and potential. His idea of the "Übermensch" (Overman) encapsulates his vision of a new kind of individual who transcends traditional moral constraints to create and live by new, life-affirming principles.

This "revaluation" aims to affirm and elevate human potential, vitality, and creativity, rather than conform to outdated, life-denying moral frameworks (Nietzsche, Thus Spoke Zarathustra, 1883–1885). Nietzsche envisioned a society where individuals are empowered to forge their own paths and create their own values, free from the constraints of conventional morality.

Critique of Metaphysics: Nietzsche's critique extends beyond morality to encompass metaphysical concepts such as absolute truth and objective reality. He argued that these notions are illusions created by humans to manage the uncertainties and complexities of existence. Nietzsche challenged the idea of an objective reality that exists independently of human perception, suggesting that reality is a construct shaped by individual perspectives and interpretations. He postulated that the search for absolute truths and universal certainties is ultimately futile, as our understanding of the world is always mediated through subjective experiences and interpretations (Nietzsche, The Gay Science, 1882). Nietzsche's declaration that "God is dead" reflects his belief that traditional metaphysical and religious frameworks are no longer tenable in the modern world and that new frameworks must be developed to navigate existence in a more authentic and empowered manner.

Impact on Modern Thought: Nietzsche's critique of traditional values largely impacts contemporary philosophy, psychology, and cultural theory. His ideas influenced existentialism, particularly the works of Jean-Paul Sartre and Albert Camus, who grappled with themes of meaning, authenticity, and individual freedom in the absence of absolute truths. His thoughts on power, will, and the creation of values have informed various fields, including political theory, literature, and psychoanalysis. His philosophy continues to provoke discussions about the nature of existence, the role of morality, and the limits of human knowledge.

2. THE CONCEPT OF NIHILISM AND THE "DEATH OF GOD"

Nihilism is a central theme in Friedrich Nietzsche's philosophy, representing a profound crisis of meaning and value in the modern world. This concept is intricately linked to Nietzsche's declaration of the "death of God," which marks a significant turning point in his critique of traditional values and metaphysical beliefs.

The "Death of God": Nietzsche's proclamation that "God is dead" in The Gay Science serves as a metaphor for the collapse of traditional religious and metaphysical frameworks that had long provided meaning, purpose, and moral guidance to human life. The "death of God" reflects a profound shift in Western thought, where the belief in an omnipotent deity and a universal moral order is no longer tenable in the face of modern scientific understanding and philosophical skepticism. Nietzsche's declaration is not a literal claim about the existence of God but rather an acknowledgment of the erosion of religious authority and the subsequent vacuum in moral and existential certainty (Nietzsche, The Gay Science, 1882). This loss leads to a state of existential disorientation and confusion as the traditional sources of meaning are revealed to be insufficient or illusory.

Nihilism Defined: Nihilism arises from the realization that the decline of religious and metaphysical certainties has left a void where traditional values and purposes once stood. It is characterized by a profound sense of meaninglessness and despair as individuals confront the absence of absolute truths and moral anchors. In this nihilistic condition, the foundational beliefs that structured and justified human life are seen as untenable or irrelevant. Nihilism thus represents the consequence of the "death of God" and the broader crisis of value that accompanies it. Nietzsche describes this condition as one in which formerly accepted beliefs and values are critically examined or outright rejected, resulting in a period of existential uncertainty and disillusionment (Nietzsche, The Will to Power, 1901).

Implications for Humanity: The impact of nihilism on human experience is both profound and multifaceted. On one hand, nihilism presents a crisis, forcing individuals to confront the inherent meaninglessness of existence and the collapse of traditional moral frameworks. This confrontation can lead to feelings of despair, futility, and existential angst. On the other hand, Nietzsche saw nihilism as an opportunity for creative transformation and value creation. He believed that the absence of pre-given meanings and values opens up the possibility for individuals to forge their own paths, invent new values, and reshape their lives according to their own principles. In this sense, nihilism is not merely a crisis but also a chance to transcend the old order and embrace a more authentic, self-determined existence (Nietzsche, The Will to Power, 1901).

Nihilism and the Übermensch: Nietzsche's concept of the Übermensch emerges as a response to the nihilistic crisis. The Übermensch embodies Nietzsche's vision of a life-affirming philosophy that embraces the freedom and responsibility of value creation. The Übermensch is an ideal for overcoming nihilism by embodying strength, creativity, and the will to shape one's destiny (Nietzsche, Thus Spoke Zarathustra, 1883–1885).

Nihilism and Cultural Critique: Nietzsche's exploration of

nihilism also extends to a critique of contemporary culture and its values. He observed that the decline of religious and metaphysical certainties was not only a personal or philosophical issue but also a cultural phenomenon. Nietzsche's critique of modernity involves examining how societal norms, values, and institutions have been affected by the loss of traditional foundations. He challenged contemporary cultural practices that, in his view, perpetuated a form of nihilism by failing to address or resolve the underlying crisis of meaning (Nietzsche, The Birth of Tragedy, 1872).

Contemporary Relevance: The concept of nihilism and the "death of God" continue to resonate in modern philosophical and cultural discussions. Nietzsche's insights into the crisis of meaning and the need for new value creation remain relevant as individuals and societies grapple with the challenges of existential uncertainty. The ongoing relevance of Nietzsche's ideas can be seen in debates about secularism, the role of religion, and the search for meaning in a rapidly changing world.

3. NIETZSCHE'S SOLUTION: THE ÜBERMENSCH AND THE CREATION OF PERSONAL VALUES

In response to the crisis of nihilism and the collapse of traditional values, Friedrich Nietzsche proposed the concept of the "Übermensch" as a solution.

The Übermensch Concept: The Übermensch is central to Nietzsche's philosophy. Unlike individuals bound by traditional moral constraints, the Übermensch is characterized by their ability to overcome societal norms and create new values and meanings for themselves. This figure is seen as the pinnacle of human evolution, achieving a state of self-mastery and creativity that transcends the limitations imposed by conventional ethics and metaphysical beliefs. The Übermensch embraces life in its fullness, including its inherent challenges and contradictions, and is not bound by the dichotomy of good and evil as traditionally defined (Nietzsche, Thus Spoke Zarathustra, 1883–1885).

Creation of Personal Values: Nietzsche's philosophy advocates creating personal values as a response to the nihilistic void left by the "death of God." Rather than adhering to externally imposed norms and values, individuals are encouraged to actively engage in the process of self-creation and value formation. This involves a profound rejection of traditional moral constraints, which Nietzsche views as life-denying and restrictive. Instead, individuals should embrace personal authenticity and individuality, creating values that reflect their own unique experiences, desires, and aspirations. Nietzsche argues that true freedom and meaning come from the ability to shape one's values and live in accordance with them, thus affirming life and one's creative potential

(Nietzsche, Beyond Good and Evil, 1886).

The creation of personal values is not merely an intellectual exercise but a practical endeavor that requires individuals to confront and overcome their limitations and societal expectations.

Eternal Recurrence: Another central concept in Nietzsche's philosophy is the idea of eternal recurrence, which serves as both a thought experiment and a test of life-affirming commitment. Eternal recurrence proposes that one should live as if they would have to relive their life repeatedly, infinitely. This concept challenges individuals to consider whether they would be willing to repeat their lives with all its joys, sorrows, and experiences. By embracing this idea, individuals are encouraged to live authentically and with full engagement, creating meaning and values they would find worthy of repeating eternally. "Eternal recurrence" is designed to inspire a life of intentionality and self-affirmation, where each moment and choice is made with the awareness of its potential eternal repetition (Nietzsche, The Gay Science, 1882). This concept reinforces Nietzsche's emphasis on living a life that reflects one's deepest values and aspirations and serves as a measure of one's ability to embrace and affirm one's existence.

Role of Art and Creativity: Nietzsche also emphasizes the role of art and creativity in the life of the Übermensch. For him, art is not merely a form of aesthetic pleasure but a vital means of expressing and affirming life's inherent complexities and contradictions. The Übermensch engages with the world artistically, using creativity to shape and redefine values and meanings. Art allows individuals to transcend mundane existence and engage with life in a way that reflects their deepest inner drives and aspirations. This artistic approach to life is seen as a way to overcome nihilism and create a sense of purpose and fulfillment in the absence of traditional structures (Nietzsche, The Birth of Tragedy, 1872).

Nietzsche's Influence on Existentialism: Existentialist philosophers, such as Jean-Paul Sartre and Albert Camus, have drawn on Nietzsche's concepts to explore themes of individual freedom, self-creation, and the search for meaning in a world devoid of intrinsic purpose. Nietzsche's emphasis on personal responsibility and the creation of values resonates with existentialist ideas about the role of individual choice and authenticity in shaping one's existence.

Criticisms and Interpretations: Nietzsche's concept of the Übermensch and his broader philosophical ideas have been subject to various interpretations and criticisms. Some critics argue that Nietzsche's vision of the Übermensch is elitist or overly individualistic, potentially overlooking the social and communal dimensions of human existence. Others have debated the practical implications of Nietzsche's call for personal value creation and its feasibility in contemporary social and ethical challenges.

Despite these criticisms, Nietzsche's ideas continue to provoke thoughtful discussion and debate, reflecting their enduring relevance and complexity. His solution to the crisis of meaning and values in the modern world involves the concept of the "Übermensch" and the creation of personal values.

By transcending traditional moralities and embracing the challenge of self-overcoming, individuals can create new, life-affirming principles that reflect their unique potential and creativity.

In conclusion, Nietzsche's critique of traditional values and his exploration of nihilism serve as a profound challenge to inherited systems of meaning, morality, and truth. Confronting the existential void left by the "death of God," Nietzsche does not advocate despair but calls for a radical reimagining of human life through the figure of the Übermensch. This ideal represents the potential for self-overcoming, value creation, and life affirmation in the absence of absolute truths. By embracing personal authenticity, creativity, and the eternal recurrence, individuals are invited to forge new paths grounded in strength, vitality, and purpose. Nietzsche's philosophy ultimately offers not a final answer, but a powerful invitation to live courageously in a world without guarantees—one where meaning must be created, not discovered.

CHAPTER 3
EXISTENTIALISM AND THE INDIVIDUAL'S RESPONSE

1. OVERVIEW OF EXISTENTIALISM AS A RESPONSE TO MEANINGLESSNESS

EXISTENTIALISM, a philosophical movement that emerged in the early 20th century, confronts the problem of meaning and the individual's role in a world perceived as devoid of intrinsic purpose. This philosophical tradition explores the nature of existence, freedom, and the search for personal meaning amid the meaninglessness of life.

Central Themes

Subjective Experience: Existentialism emphasizes the subjective experience of the individual. It highlights the importance of personal perspective and the unique ways individuals confront and interpret their existence. According to existentialist thinkers, individuals are not just passive recipients of meaning but active creators of their own values and purpose.

Absurdity: A key theme in existentialism is absurdism, which describes the conflict between humans' search for intrinsic purpose and the universe's indifference. Albert Camus has explored how individuals can confront the absurd condition without resorting to despair or nihilism (see Chapter 1).

Alienation: Existentialism also addresses feelings of alienation, the sense of estrangement from the world or oneself that arises when traditional sources of meaning (such as religion, societal norms, or ideology) fail to provide satisfactory answers. This alienation underscores the struggle to find meaning in a seemingly indifferent universe.

Freedom and Responsibility: Existentialist philosophy places a significant emphasis on individual freedom and responsibility. It asserts that, in the absence of predetermined meaning, individuals are free to create their own values and meaning through their choices and actions. Jean-Paul Sartre, in Being and Nothingness, argues that freedom is both a gift and a burden, as it requires individuals to take full responsibility for their lives and the meanings they construct.

Authenticity: Authenticity, or living in accordance with one's true self, is another central existentialist theme. Existentialists argue that to live authentically is to act in ways that align with one's values and beliefs rather than conforming to societal expectations or external pressures. This pursuit of authenticity is seen as a path to personal fulfillment and self-realization.

Philosophical Context

Reaction to Rationalism and Scientific Approaches: Existentialism arose partly due to the perceived limitations of rationalist and scientific approaches to understanding human existence. Existentialists argue that the search for objective, universal meanings, as pursued by rationalist and scientific methodologies, fails to capture the depth of human experience. Existentialism rejects the idea that external, objective sources can provide the ultimate answers to questions of meaning.

Emphasis on Personal Engagement: Instead, existentialism asserts that meaning is a product of personal engagement and individual choice. Martin Heidegger, in Being and Time, explores the nature of being and the importance of personal experience in constructing meaning. Heidegger's focus on "Being" underscores the existentialist belief that meaning arises from the lived experience of individuals rather than from abstract, universal principles.

Influence and Legacy

Literature and Arts: Existentialism has profoundly influenced literature and the arts. Writers such as Franz Kafka, Fyodor Dostoevsky, and Virginia Woolf have explored existential themes in their works, depicting characters grappling with issues of meaning, freedom, and alienation. The existentialist emphasis on individual experience and subjective reality has had a lasting impact on contemporary narrative forms and artistic expressions.

Psychology and Cultural Criticism: Existentialism has also influenced fields such as psychology and cultural criticism.

In psychology, existentialist ideas have informed approaches to therapy that focus on helping individuals find personal meaning and confront existential concerns. Cultural critics have used existentialist concepts to analyze and critique modern societal issues, such as the search for identity in a rapidly changing world.

Contemporary Issues: The existentialist emphasis on personal responsibility, authenticity, and self-creation resonates with various contemporary issues, including individualism, moral relativism, and the search for identity in a globalized and often fragmented world. The existentialist perspective continues to offer valuable insights into the challenges of navigating modern life and finding personal meaning.

Overall, existentialism provides a framework for understanding and addressing the complexities of human existence. Its focus on subjective experience, freedom, and personal responsibility offers a compelling response to the challenges of meaninglessness.

2. KEY FIGURES: JEAN-PAUL SARTRE, SIMONE DE BEAUVOIR, AND THEIR CONTRIBUTIONS

Existentialism is defined by the contributions of several key figures, with Jean-Paul Sartre and Simone de Beauvoir standing out for their profound impact on the philosophy. Their works not only explore fundamental existential themes but also expand the discussion to address issues of freedom, responsibility, and social structures.

Jean-Paul Sartre

Central Contributions: Jean-Paul Sartre stands as a central figure in existentialist philosophy, celebrated for his exploration of freedom, responsibility, and the nature of human existence. His influential work Being and Nothingness (1943) outlines a foundational existentialist framework, centered on the idea that "existence precedes essence." This concept rejects the notion that individuals possess a fixed, preordained nature or purpose. Instead, Sartre argues that people define themselves and create meaning through their actions, choices, and engagement with the world.

Concept of Freedom: Sartre's existentialism emphasizes radical freedom, the idea that individuals are entirely free to make their own choices. This freedom, however, comes with the burden of responsibility, as individuals must confront the full weight of their choices and the consequences that follow. Sartre explores how this radical freedom leads to feelings of anxiety and responsibility, as individuals are not only responsible for their own actions but also for defining the essence of what it means to be human.

Bad Faith: A central concept in Sartre's existential

philosophy is bad faith (mauvaise foi), which refers to the human tendency to flee from the burden of freedom by engaging in self-deception or uncritically adopting societal roles. Bad faith occurs when individuals deny their inherent freedom and responsibility by conforming to external expectations, thereby avoiding the existential anxiety that accompanies authentic self-realization. For Sartre, this self-deception is a form of lying to oneself—choosing not to recognize one's radical freedom and the responsibility it entails.

Existentialism as a Humanism: In his 1946 lecture Existentialism Is a Humanism, Jean-Paul Sartre responds to criticisms that existentialism is pessimistic or nihilistic. He argues that, on the contrary, existentialism is profoundly optimistic because it affirms human freedom and the ability to create one's own values and meaning. Sartre's existentialism emphasizes the transformative power of human choice, the potential for personal growth, and the responsibility of individuals to define themselves through their actions.

Simone de Beauvoir

Central Contributions: Simone de Beauvoir, a prominent existentialist and pioneering feminist philosopher, is best known for her groundbreaking work The Second Sex (1949). In this text, she examines the existential dimensions of women's oppression and the construction of female identity within patriarchal society. De Beauvoir extends existentialist principles into the domain of gender and social structures, analyzing how women have been historically marginalized and positioned as "the Other" in relation to men.

Existential Oppression and Liberation: Simone de Beauvoir contends that women have been systematically oppressed by being defined in relation to men, rather than as autonomous individuals. She exposes how societal norms and rigid gender roles constrain women's freedom and hinder authentic self-definition. De Beauvoir emphasizes the existential importance of self-determination and personal freedom as essential means for overcoming these limitations and achieving a more authentic and liberated existence.

The Notion of the "Other": One of de Beauvoir's key contributions is her analysis of the concept of the "Other." She examines how women have been historically positioned as the "Other" in relation to the male "Self," leading to their marginalization and objectification. De Beauvoir argues that women must challenge and transcend these imposed roles to reclaim their freedom and authenticity.

Intersection with Sartre's Thought: De Beauvoir's existentialist feminism complements Sartre's theories by addressing the specific existential struggles women face.

Their collaborative relationship and intellectual exchange significantly shaped their respective works. De Beauvoir's focus on gender and social constraints intersects with Sartre's ideas on freedom and responsibility, highlighting how societal expectations can impact one's ability to live authentically.

Influence and Intersection

Collaboration and Personal Relationship: Sartre and de Beauvoir's collaboration and personal relationship were instrumental in shaping existentialist thought. Their mutual influence is evident in their shared focus on themes of freedom, authenticity, and the challenge of living an authentic life amidst societal expectations. Their works often intersect, as seen in their discussions on how social structures and personal freedom intertwine.

Impact on Existentialist Thought: Sartre's emphasis on radical freedom and responsibility complements de Beauvoir's analysis of gender oppression and the construction of identity. Together, their works provide a comprehensive exploration of existentialist themes, addressing both individual and social dimensions of freedom and authenticity.

Contemporary Relevance: The existentialist ideas advanced by Sartre and de Beauvoir continue to resonate in contemporary discussions. Their insights into the nature of existence, the struggle for authenticity, and the impact of societal structures remain relevant in addressing modern issues related to gender, identity, and individual responsibility.

Overall, Sartre and de Beauvoir's contributions to existentialism offer profound insights into the nature of human freedom and responsibility, and their works continue to influence philosophical and social thought.

3. THE ROLE OF FREEDOM AND RESPONSIBILITY IN CRAFTING PERSONAL MEANING

A cornerstone of existentialist philosophy is the emphasis on freedom and responsibility as fundamental to creating personal meaning. Existentialists assert that, in the absence of intrinsic purpose in the universe, individuals must confront and embrace their freedom to shape their lives and find significance through their own actions.

Radical Freedom

Definition and Scope: Existentialism suggests that human beings possess radical freedom and profound autonomy to choose their actions and define their own essence. This concept of radical freedom extends beyond mere decision-making to encompass a deeper engagement with one's potential and the implications of one's choices. It implies that predetermined natures or external authorities do not bind individuals; rather, they are the architects of their own lives.

Empowerment and Anxiety: The realization of radical freedom is a double-edged sword—simultaneously empowering and anxiety-inducing. On one hand, it grants individuals the capacity to shape their own destinies and create personal meaning. On the other, it introduces existential anxiety, as the weight of absolute responsibility can be overwhelming. Jean-Paul Sartre, in Being and Nothingness (1943), explores how this freedom is inherently tied to a profound sense of responsibility, often resulting in feelings of dread or existential angst when faced with the task of making meaningful, authentic choices.

Responsibility and authenticity

Responsibility: With freedom comes the weight of responsibility. Existentialists argue that individuals are free to make choices and are responsible for the values they create and the meanings they derive from their lives. This responsibility involves acknowledging that one's actions and decisions define one's essence and affect others. For example, Sartre's notion of "bad faith" illustrates how individuals might evade this responsibility by conforming to societal norms or roles, thus denying their freedom.

Authenticity: Authenticity involves living in accordance with one's true self and values rather than conforming to external expectations or societal norms. According to existentialist philosophy, living authentically means embracing one's freedom and making choices that reflect one's genuine desires and beliefs. Martin Heidegger, in Being and Time (1927), asserts that authenticity arises when individuals confront the inevitability of their own death and the transient nature of existence. This confrontation serves as a call to live genuinely—shaping one's life according to personal conviction rather than conforming to societal expectations or external pressures.

Creating Meaning

Active Engagement: In a world perceived as devoid of intrinsic purpose, existentialist thinkers argue that individuals must take responsibility for creating their own purpose. This process of meaning-making involves setting personal goals, pursuing passions, and cultivating relationships that align with one's values. Albert Camus, in The Myth of Sisyphus (1942), contends that even within an indifferent universe, individuals can discover meaning by embracing their condition and finding joy in the very act of living and striving—much like Sisyphus, who finds fulfillment in his eternal task.

Self-Creation: Creating meaning is a dynamic process that involves self-creation. Existentialists suggest that individuals can craft meaningful lives by taking ownership of their choices and actions. This process of self-creation is not about achieving some ultimate purpose but about finding significance in the act of living and engaging with life's experiences.

"Existential Angst and Overcoming"

Existential Angst: The awareness of one's radical freedom and responsibility often leads to existential angst—a profound sense of dread or anxiety about the burden of creating meaning in a seemingly indifferent world. This angst arises from the realization that individuals must confront the void of intrinsic purpose and the full weight of their choices.

Overcoming Angst: Existentialists argue that this angst is a natural part of the human condition and can be mitigated by embracing one's freedom and engaging authentically with life. Sartre and Camus suggest that individuals can overcome existential angst by accepting their freedom, taking responsibility for their choices, and finding personal fulfillment through authentic engagement with their own values and passions.

In summary, existentialism offers a framework for addressing the perceived meaninglessness of life by emphasizing the role of individual freedom and responsibility. Key figures, such as Jean-Paul Sartre and Simone de Beauvoir, provide crucial insights into how individuals can confront existential challenges and create their own meaning through personal choices and authentic engagement with their existence.

PART TWO
SCIENTIFIC PERSPECTIVES ON EXISTENCE

CHAPTER 4
EVOLUTIONARY BIOLOGY AND THE MEANING OF LIFE

1. CHARLES DARWIN'S THEORY OF EVOLUTION AND ITS IMPLICATIONS FOR EXISTENTIAL THOUGHT

CHARLES DARWIN'S SEMINAL WORK, On the Origin of Species (1859), introduced the theory of evolution by natural selection, which fundamentally reshaped our understanding of life's complexity and origin. Darwin's theory proposes that species evolve over time through a process driven by natural selection, in which advantageous traits that enhance survival and reproduction become more common in successive generations.

This process operates through random genetic variations and environmental pressures rather than through any predetermined or purposeful design. Darwin's theory shifted the perspective from a creationist or teleological view of life to one grounded in natural processes and scientific inquiry.

Implications for Existential Thought: Darwin's theory challenges traditional notions of intrinsic purpose or purpose in life. By framing evolution as a random and non-teleological process, Darwin's work suggests that life's complexity and diversity are the result of natural forces rather than intentional design. This view resonates with existentialist themes that question the existence of intrinsic meaning in the universe. The idea that life evolves through random mutations and survival pressures rather than through a divine or predetermined plan aligns with existentialist thought, which emphasizes the absence of an intrinsic purpose and the need for individuals to create their own meaning. This naturalistic perspective contributes to a more secular worldview, where meaning is not derived from a higher order but from human experience and personal choice (Dennett, Darwin's Dangerous Idea, 1995).

Impact on Human Self-Understanding: Darwin's theory has profound implications for how humans perceive themselves in the grand scheme of existence. By demonstrating that humans are products of evolutionary processes rather than unique or privileged beings, Darwin's work compels a profound re-evaluation of human significance and purpose. It challenges anthropocentric worldviews that place humanity at the center of creation, instead presenting human existence as part of a vast, indifferent natural process. This shift in perspective invites existential reflection on the nature of human life and its place in the universe. It emphasizes that humans, like all living organisms, are governed by the same natural forces of evolution and survival. Such a realization may lead to a deeper questioning of traditional narratives that assign special meaning or divine purpose to human life (Gould, The Structure of Evolutionary Theory, 2002).

2. CONCEPT OF NATURAL SELECTION AND SURVIVAL AS A DRIVING FORCE

Mechanism of Natural Selection: Natural selection operates on the premise that individuals with traits better suited to their environment are more likely to survive and reproduce. These advantageous traits become more prevalent in the population over successive generations. Natural selection is a non-random process that drives the adaptation of species to their environments, providing a powerful explanation for the emergence of complex biological traits and behaviors. For instance, the development of camouflage in prey animals or the evolution of antibiotic resistance in bacteria can be understood through this mechanism (Darwin, On the Origin of Species, 1859).

Survival as a Driving Force: In Darwinian terms, the struggle for survival and reproduction is the primary driver of evolutionary change. This concept emphasizes that life fundamentally involves adapting to environmental challenges to survive and reproduce. The focus on survival presents a view of life that prioritizes practical and immediate concerns over abstract or existential meanings. For instance, the competitive nature of survival in ecosystems, where organisms must secure resources and avoid predators, underscores the practical aspects of existence driven by biological imperatives. This perspective frames life in terms of practical survival, emphasizing that evolutionary pressures shape behaviors and traits in response to immediate survival needs (Dawkins, The Selfish Gene, 1976).

Existential Implications: The focus on survival and adaptation introduced by Darwinian evolution presents a framework where human existence is viewed through the lens of biological imperatives rather than inherent philosophical or metaphysical purposes. This perspective might suggest that the search for meaning is a human construct rather than an intrinsic aspect of existence. From an existential standpoint, this implies that meaning and value are not provided by nature but are created through individual choices and actions within the constraints of biological and environmental factors. The naturalistic view of life reinforces the idea that meaning is not preordained or derived from the natural order, but must instead be actively constructed by individuals (Wilson, The Social Conquest of Earth, 2012).

Critiques and Reflections: While natural selection provides a robust scientific explanation for the diversity of life, it has faced critiques for potentially fostering a reductionist view of human experience. Critics argue that an exclusive focus on evolutionary processes may overlook the complexities of human consciousness and the capacity for individuals to create meaning beyond mere survival and reproduction. For instance, cognitive scientists and philosophers may point out that human beings have the ability to engage in abstract reasoning, moral reflection, and cultural creation that extends beyond the survival-centric framework of evolutionary theory. This critique underscores the need for a more nuanced understanding—one that integrates evolutionary insights with the richness of human experience and the ongoing quest for meaning (Pinker, The Blank Slate, 2002).

While these concepts challenge traditional views of intrinsic purpose and meaning, they also align with existentialist perspectives that view existence as lacking intrinsic significance. The emphasis on survival and adaptation underscores a naturalistic understanding of life, prompting a reevaluation of how meaning is constructed and experienced in the absence of a predetermined purpose.

In sum, Darwin's theory of evolution by natural selection revolutionized our understanding of life by revealing a universe shaped by chance, adaptation, and survival rather than purpose or design. This perspective deeply resonates with existentialist thought, which contends that meaning is not given but made. By situating human beings within the broader continuum of life, Darwinism dismantles anthropocentric narratives and invites a humbler, more grounded reflection on our place in the cosmos. Yet rather than diminish the human experience, this view offers a liberating challenge: to create meaning in a world indifferent to it. In the face of a natural order governed by impersonal forces, the responsibility of shaping a purposeful existence lies with the individual—an existential task as daunting as it is empowering.

CHAPTER 5
THE SELFISH GENE AND DAWKINS' PERSPECTIVE

.

1. RICHARD DAWKINS' VIEW OF EVOLUTION AND THE SELFISH GENE

THE GENE-CENTERED VIEW OF EVOLUTION: Richard Dawkins' seminal work, The Selfish Gene (1976), fundamentally reshapes our understanding of evolution by emphasizing genes as the principal units of natural selection. Dawkins argues that genes, rather than individuals or species, are the primary entities selected by evolutionary pressures. This gene-centered view suggests that genes are "selfish" in the sense that they drive evolutionary processes by promoting their own replication and survival. Organisms are viewed as vehicles or "survival machines" for these genes, whose primary evolutionary goal is to propagate themselves. Dawkins' perspective shifts the focus from the fitness of individual organisms or entire species to the success of genes in replicating and spreading their genetic information across generations. By highlighting the role of genes in shaping behavior and biological traits, Dawkins provides a new framework for understanding evolution that prioritizes genetic imperatives over organismal or species-level traits (Dawkins, The Selfish Gene, 1976).

Replicators and the Evolutionary Process: In The Selfish Gene, Dawkins introduces the concept of "replicators" to explain the evolutionary process. Replicators are entities capable of making copies of themselves with variations, and genes fit this description perfectly. Dawkins argues that natural selection acts at the level of these replicators rather than focusing solely on the survival and reproduction of individual organisms or species. Genes, as replicators, undergo a selection process based on their effectiveness in copying themselves and influencing the traits and behaviors of the organisms that carry them. This shift in perspective challenges traditional evolutionary theories that center on the fitness of individual organisms or species by emphasizing how genes, as fundamental units of selection, drive evolutionary change through their influence on organismal traits and behaviors (Dawkins, The Selfish Gene, 1976).

Extended Phenotype: Dawkins's concept of the "extended phenotype," elaborated in his later work, The Extended Phenotype (1982), further expands his gene-centered view of evolution. The extended phenotype refers to the idea that the influence of genes extends beyond the physical body of the organism to affect its environment and interactions with other organisms. For example, beavers build dams, and spiders spin webs as part of their extended phenotype. These structures are not the result of individual behavior but are seen as expressions of the genes' influence on the environment. Dawkins argues that genes affect the world around the organism, shaping ecological interactions and environmental modifications in ways that enhance their own replication. This concept highlights the broader impact of genes on the ecosystem, demonstrating that evolutionary pressures and genetic influence extend beyond the organism's immediate physical form and into its interactions with the environment (Dawkins, The Extended Phenotype, 1982).

Implications for Understanding Evolution: Dawkins's gene-centered view and the concept of the extended phenotype have profound implications for how we understand evolutionary processes. By focusing on genes as the primary units of selection, Dawkins offers a perspective that emphasizes the role of genetic imperatives in shaping behavior, traits, and ecological interactions. This approach challenges traditional views, highlighting the adaptive significance of organisms or species-level traits. It also suggests that evolutionary success is measured by the effectiveness of genes in replicating and influencing their environments rather than solely by the survival and reproductive success of individual organisms.

2. HOW BIOLOGICAL IMPERATIVES CHALLENGE TRADITIONAL NOTIONS OF PURPOSE

Richard Dawkins' gene-centered view of evolution, articulated in The Selfish Gene (1976), presents a profound challenge to traditional philosophies of purpose, meaning, and morality that have often been grounded in religious, metaphysical, or teleological frameworks.

Biological Imperatives and Purpose: Dawkins' theory suggests that biological imperatives, including behaviors and traits, are fundamentally driven by the goal of gene replication rather than any intrinsic or external purpose. In this view, genes are considered "selfish" because they propagate themselves by influencing the organism's behavior and traits. This implies that what might appear to be altruistic or cooperative behaviors are actually strategies evolved to enhance the replication of genes, whether directly through kin selection or indirectly through social cooperation. This gene-centered perspective frames life as a product of mechanistic processes rather than a pursuit of intrinsic goals or cosmic order (Dawkins, The Selfish Gene, 1976).

Reductionism and Meaning: Dawkins's approach can be seen as reductionist, reducing complex behaviors and human traits to their genetic underpinnings. This view raises significant questions about the nature of purpose and meaning in human life, suggesting that such concepts may be human constructs rather than reflections of any intrinsic, universal purpose. This reductionism challenges traditional philosophical and existential views that posit meaning as inherent in the fabric of existence (Wilson, Consilience: The Unity of Knowledge, 1998).

Ethical and Philosophical Implications: The gene-centered view also has considerable implications for ethics and philosophy. If biological imperatives drive behavior, then the idea of an inherent moral purpose or cosmic order is undermined. Instead, ethical principles and values are seen as products of human culture and social evolution rather than reflections of deeper, intrinsic meaning. This perspective challenges traditional moral frameworks that rely on concepts of divine or natural purpose, suggesting that ethical norms and values are contingent on evolutionary and social contexts rather than rooted in universal truths (Nagel, The Last Word, 1997).

Critiques and Alternatives: Critics argue that while Dawkins's gene-centered perspective offers valuable insights into evolutionary processes, it may not fully account for the complexity of human consciousness, culture, and personal agency. Alternative approaches suggest that biological imperatives, while influential, do not wholly determine human meaning and purpose. Human experiences, social contexts, and personal choices also play crucial roles in shaping individual and collective understandings of purpose. For instance, ethical frameworks and personal values are often influenced by cultural, social, and existential factors beyond mere genetic imperatives (Sandel, The Case Against Perfection, 2007).

While this gene-centered perspective offers a compelling explanation of evolutionary processes, it raises significant questions about human purpose and meaning. This perspective prompts ongoing philosophical and ethical debates, highlighting the need to consider both biological imperatives and the complex interplay of individual experiences and cultural contexts in shaping human understanding of purpose.

In conclusion, Richard Dawkins' gene-centered theory of evolution radically reframes our understanding of life, behavior, and meaning by placing genetic replication at the core of evolutionary processes. By viewing organisms as vehicles for selfish genes and exploring how genetic influence extends beyond the individual through the extended phenotype, Dawkins challenges traditional, teleological, and human-centric notions of purpose. This perspective suggests that life is not guided by intrinsic goals or cosmic design but is instead the outcome of impersonal genetic imperatives. Yet, while this view may appear reductionist, it opens a vital dialogue about the origins of meaning, morality, and human agency. Rather than diminish the human experience, Dawkins' framework compels us to reconsider how meaning is constructed— inviting a deeper exploration of consciousness, culture, and ethical responsibility in a world where biology provides no built-in purpose. It is in this space between genetic determinism and existential freedom that the quest for human significance continues.

CHAPTER 6
THE UNIVERSE'S INDIFFERENCE AND THE UNIVERSE'S SCALE

1. VASTNESS OF THE UNIVERSE AND ITS IMPLICATIONS FOR HUMAN SIGNIFICANCE

THE VASTNESS of the universe offers a striking challenge to traditional notions of human significance, posing profound questions about our place and purpose in the cosmos. This grand scale and the dynamic nature of cosmic phenomena prompt reflections on the relative importance of human life in the broader context of the universe.

Cosmic Scale: The observable universe, spanning approximately 93 billion light-years in diameter, contains an extraordinary number of celestial bodies. It is home to hundreds of billions of galaxies, each comprising millions to billions of stars—and potentially countless planets (NASA, 2023).

This immense scale puts human achievements and concerns into stark perspective, revealing the relatively minuscule nature of human existence in the grand cosmic scheme. The enormity of the universe often evokes a sense of the universe's indifference, where individual human lives and endeavors seem insignificant when viewed against the backdrop of the universe's vastness complexity (Hawking, A Brief History of Time, 1988).

Astronomical Discoveries: Modern astronomy has revealed the vast scale of the universe and illustrated its dynamic and ever-changing nature. Discoveries, such as the detection of exoplanets, the analysis of cosmic microwave background radiation, and the observation of distant galaxies have expanded our understanding of the universe's scale and history. These findings underscore the immense distances and timescales involved, emphasizing the contrast between human lifespans and the universe's ancient and ongoing processes. The continuous discovery of new cosmic phenomena challenges our previous perceptions and highlights the ever-expanding nature of our cosmic knowledge (Kipling, Cosmos, 2011).

Implications for Human Significance: Recognizing the immense scale and complexity of the universe can provoke deep existential reflections on human significance. The realization that Earth is just a tiny, unremarkable planet in a vast and seemingly indifferent cosmos challenges anthropocentric views, which place humanity at the center of the universe's purpose and meaning. This perspective often leads to feelings of humility and existential anxiety as individuals grapple with the apparent lack of a central or privileged place for humanity in the cosmic order. The vastness of the universe can prompt individuals to question traditional beliefs about human purpose and seek new ways to find meaning in a context that seems indifferent to our existence (Sagan, Pale Blue Dot, 1994).

Philosophical and Existential Reflections: The vastness of the universe and our place within it invite philosophical and existential reflections on human purpose.

Philosophers and thinkers have explored how to reconcile the apparent insignificance of human life with the quest for meaning. Some argue that while the universe may be indifferent to human existence, individuals can create their own meaning through personal achievements, relationships, and contributions to society. This existential perspective emphasizes the importance of personal agency and the capacity to find significance within the framework of an indifferent universe.

Cultural and Psychological Impacts: The awareness of our cosmic insignificance can have varied cultural and psychological impacts. For some, it may lead to a sense of nihilism or despair, while others might find inspiration in the pursuit of knowledge and the exploration of our place in the universe. The recognition of our smallness in the grand cosmic scheme can also foster a sense of unity and interconnectedness as individuals and societies confront their shared existence within the vast expanse of the cosmos.

These reflections prompt individuals to explore new ways of finding meaning and significance through personal achievements, philosophical contemplation, or a deeper understanding of our place within the cosmos.

2. SCIENTIFIC PERSPECTIVES ON COSMIC INSIGNIFICANCE AND HUMAN EXISTENCE

Scientific perspectives on cosmic insignificance explore how our understanding of the universe challenges traditional views on human centrality and purpose. These insights, drawn from cosmology, astrophysics, and evolutionary theory, offer profound implications for philosophical and existential reflections on the meaning of life.

the universe's indifference: Scientific discoveries in cosmology and astrophysics reveal a universe that operates according to natural laws and processes that are indifferent to human concerns. This notion of the universe's indifference suggests that the universe itself does not possess any intrinsic purpose or moral direction. Instead, human existence is seen as a byproduct of random events and natural processes rather than the result of divine or predetermined plans (Penrose, The Road to Reality, 2004). The vast and impersonal nature of cosmic phenomena—such as the formation and behavior of galaxies, stars, and other celestial bodies—reinforces the idea that the universe functions independently of human values or aspirations. This perspective can evoke a sense of existential humility and challenge anthropocentric views that place human life at the center of cosmic significance.

Evolutionary Cosmology: Theories such as the Big Bang and cosmic inflation describe the universe's origins and its subsequent evolution. According to these models, the universe began as a singularity and has been expanding and evolving according to physical laws and probabilistic events. This dynamic and ever-changing universe, governed by fundamental forces such as gravity and quantum mechanics, does not inherently regard human significance (Hawking, The Grand Design, 2010). Evolutionary cosmology illustrates that humans result from a long evolutionary process within a vast and complex universe. This understanding challenges notions of a particular or privileged status for humanity, emphasizing that our existence is part of a broader, impersonal cosmic process rather than a result of unique or exceptional circumstances.

Anthropic Principle: The anthropic principle addresses the apparent fine-tuning of the universe for the existence of life. It suggests that the physical constants of the universe are such that they allow for the emergence of life as we know it. Some interpretations of the anthropic principle propose that the fundamental properties of the universe appear finely tuned for human existence, suggesting a form of design or special suitability (Carr & Rees, The Anthropic Principle, 1979).

However, alternative views argue that fine-tuning could be a statistical necessity given the vast number of potential universes or conditions that could have existed. This principle underscores the tension between the apparent uniqueness of our universe and the broader context of the universe's indifference, highlighting how scientific explanations can both support and challenge traditional notions of purpose.

Philosophical Reflections: While the universe may be indifferent to human concerns, philosophers and existentialists argue that individuals must find or create their own meaning and purpose through personal experiences and choices. Albert Camus explores the concept of existential absurdity in The Myth of Sisyphus (1942), arguing that even in a universe devoid of intrinsic purpose, individuals can attain a sense of fulfillment by consciously embracing the absurd and actively engaging in their lives. Rather than succumbing to despair, this acknowledgment of the universe's indifference can deepen one's appreciation of human agency and creativity. Camus encourages individuals to forge meaning through their actions, relationships, and personal accomplishments— without relying on external or metaphysical validation.

Impact on Human Values and Ethics: The recognition of cosmic insignificance also has implications for human values and ethics. Without a universal or divine purpose, ethical principles and moral values may be viewed as constructs of human culture and social evolution. This perspective suggests that values are created and negotiated through human interactions and societal development rather than being inherent or predetermined. It challenges traditional moral frameworks that rely on notions of a higher cosmic order or divine command, emphasizing instead the role of human responsibility in defining ethical standards and guiding behavior.

Cultural and Psychological Effects: The awareness of our cosmic insignificance can have diverse cultural and psychological effects. For some, it may lead to existential anxiety or nihilism; for others, it may inspire a sense of liberation and empowerment. Recognizing our small place in the vast universe can foster a sense of unity with others, encouraging collective efforts to address global challenges and promote shared human values. It can also prompt individuals to find personal significance and purpose through creative endeavors, personal growth, and contributions to the broader human community.

Scientific perspectives on cosmic insignificance provide a transformative lens for understanding human existence. These views challenge traditional notions of human centrality and purpose by revealing a universe that operates independently of human concerns and emphasizing its vastness and dynamic nature. The concept of the universe's indifference highlights the relative smallness of human life within the grand cosmic scheme. This perspective underscores the need for philosophical and existential reflection on how individuals and societies can create their own significance in an indifferent universe. Rather than seeking meaning through cosmic affirmation, these insights encourage us to shape our lives through personal choices, ethical principles, and cultural contributions.

In conclusion, the staggering scale and impersonal nature of the universe pose a profound challenge to traditional notions of human centrality and purpose. Scientific discoveries in cosmology and astrophysics underscore a cosmos that operates without regard for human concerns —a universe vast, ancient, and indifferent. This realization invites both existential humility and philosophical reflection, prompting us to grapple with the implications of our apparent insignificance. Yet, in facing the void of the universe's indifference, we are also offered a unique opportunity: to forge meaning not from the stars, but from within ourselves. Human significance need not be derived from external validation; it can emerge through the exercise of agency, the cultivation of values, and the pursuit of shared understanding. In embracing our smallness, we may come to appreciate the fragile beauty of consciousness and the collective power of human creativity. It is within this tension—between the scale of the universe and the depth of human experience—that we find the space to define our own purpose.

CHAPTER 7
THE LIMITS OF SCIENTIFIC UNDERSTANDING

1. BOUNDARIES OF SCIENCE IN ADDRESSING EXISTENTIAL QUESTIONS

WHILE SCIENCE HAS ACHIEVED remarkable progress in elucidating the natural world, it encounters inherent limitations when addressing existential questions concerning meaning, purpose, and the human condition. These boundaries stem from the nature of scientific inquiry and the scope of its methodologies.

Nature of Scientific Inquiry: Science operates on empirical foundations, focusing on observation, experimentation, and evidence to uncover objective truths about physical phenomena. By formulating hypotheses, conducting experiments, and analyzing data, science excels at understanding natural processes and establishing causal relationships. However, this empirical approach is less suited to exploring subjective realms, such as personal meaning and individual purpose. Questions related to existential significance often lie outside the purview of empirical methods, requiring different modes of inquiry that go beyond measurable phenomena (Popper, The Logic of Scientific Discovery, 1959).

Existential and Metaphysical Questions: Existential questions, such as those concerning the meaning of life, the nature of consciousness, and the existence of value, delve into areas that transcend empirical observation. These inquiries often involve subjective experiences, ethical considerations, and philosophical reflections that cannot be easily quantified or measured. While science can provide insights into the mechanisms of life and consciousness, it does not necessarily address the more profound philosophical and metaphysical dimensions of human experience. These aspects are typically explored through philosophy, theology, and personal reflection, which offer perspectives beyond the empirical (Nagel, The View from Nowhere,1986).

Scientific Reductionism: Scientific reductionism seeks to understand complex phenomena by analyzing their fundamental components. While this approach has advanced our knowledge significantly, it may lead to a reductionist view that neglects the holistic aspects of human experience. For instance, understanding the brain's neural processes offers insights into cognitive functions but does not fully capture the subjective experience of consciousness or the qualitative aspects of the self. This limitation highlights the difficulty of addressing questions that involve the full richness and depth of human experience—questions that demand integrative approaches combining both empirical evidence and existential insight (Wilson, Consilience: The Unity of Knowledge, 1998).

2. ROLE OF SCIENTIFIC INQUIRY IN UNDERSTANDING THE HUMAN CONDITION

Despite its limitations in addressing existential questions, scientific inquiry plays a pivotal role in enhancing our understanding of the human condition. By providing insights into human biology, psychology, and behavior, science contributes valuable knowledge that informs philosophical and existential reflections.

Biological and Psychological Insights: Advances in fields such as genetics, neurobiology, and psychology have significantly deepened our understanding of the biological and cognitive dimensions of human experience. For example, research into the brain's structure and function has illuminated the neurological underpinnings of emotions, decision-making processes, and consciousness. Studies in evolutionary psychology offer explanations for how specific behavioral patterns and cognitive functions may have evolved to address survival and reproductive challenges. These scientific insights help clarify aspects of human nature, mental health, and social interactions, providing a foundation for further philosophical exploration (Damasio, Descartes' Error, 1994).

Impact on Philosophy and Ethics: The intersection of scientific discoveries with philosophical and ethical questions enriches our comprehension of complex issues related to human existence. For instance, understanding the genetic and neurobiological bases of behaviors can influence debates about free will, moral responsibility, and personal identity. Insights from scientific research challenge and refine traditional philosophical concepts, prompting reevaluations of ethical frameworks and the nature of human agency. The integration of scientific knowledge with philosophical discourse offers a more nuanced perspective on the moral and existential dimensions of human life (Pinker, The Better Angels of Our Nature, 2011).

Interdisciplinary Approaches: Addressing existential questions effectively often requires an interdisciplinary approach that combines scientific, philosophical, and experiential perspectives. Cognitive science and the philosophy of mind work together to explore questions about consciousness and self-awareness, merging empirical findings with theoretical analysis. Bioethics examines the implications of scientific advancements for ethical decision-making and human values, integrating scientific knowledge with ethical considerations. These interdisciplinary efforts underscore the importance of synthesizing scientific insights with broader philosophical and experiential contexts to address the multifaceted nature of human existence (Sandel, The Case Against Perfection, 2007).

Limitations and Future Directions: While science contributes substantially to our understanding of the human condition, it is essential to recognize its limitations and the need for continued exploration. Future research endeavors may bridge the gap between empirical knowledge and existential inquiry, fostering a more comprehensive understanding of the human experience. This includes investigating how biological, psychological, and cultural factors shape meaning and personal significance. Continued interdisciplinary collaboration and exploration will be essential in advancing our grasp of the complexities of human existence and the pursuit of meaning (Eagleman, Incognito: The Secret Lives of the Brain, 2011).

While science offers profound insights into the natural world and human biology, it faces inherent limitations in addressing existential questions about meaning and purpose. The empirical nature of scientific inquiry is well-suited to understanding physical phenomena but may not fully capture the subjective and philosophical dimensions of human existence. Nevertheless, scientific inquiry plays a crucial role in enhancing our understanding of the human condition by providing valuable insights into the biological and cognitive aspects of experience. These insights intersect with philosophical and ethical discussions, highlighting the importance of interdisciplinary approaches. Acknowledging the limitations of science, ongoing research, and collaboration can contribute to a richer and more nuanced understanding of human existence and meaning.

In sum, while science remains one of humanity's most powerful tools for uncovering the workings of the natural world, it is not equipped to fully address the deeper existential questions that define the human experience. The empirical scope of scientific inquiry excels at explaining mechanisms and uncovering causal relationships; yet it often falls short when grappling with the subjective, the metaphysical, and the moral dimensions of life. Questions of meaning, purpose, and value resist reduction to data points or laboratory results, instead requiring philosophical reflection, ethical deliberation, and personal insight. Nonetheless, scientific knowledge profoundly enriches our understanding of the human condition, especially when integrated with perspectives from philosophy, theology, and the arts. The limitations of science need not be seen as shortcomings, but rather as invitations to broader, interdisciplinary exploration. By acknowledging these boundaries while embracing science's contributions, we move closer to a holistic understanding of what it means to be human—one that honors both the empirical and the existential dimensions of our lives.

PART THREE
NAVIGATING
MEANINGLESSNESS

CHAPTER 8
EMBRACING THE ABSURD: CAMUS'S APPROACH

1. CONCEPT OF LIVING WITHOUT APPEAL TO HIGHER MEANING

ALBERT CAMUS'S philosophy of the absurd challenges traditional views that seek to find or impose cosmic or metaphysical significance on human existence. His approach to embracing the absurd offers a way to navigate this existential realization without resorting to nihilism or despair.

Absurdism Defined: According to Camus, the absurd arises from the confrontation between humans' innate desire for meaning and the universe's indifferent silence. This clash produces a sense of disillusionment as individuals come to terms with the fact that the universe does not offer intrinsic purpose or purpose. For Camus, recognizing the absurd is a crucial step in understanding the human condition and deciding how to live authentically within it (Camus, The Myth of Sisyphus, 1942). The absurd is not a fleeting realization but a fundamental aspect of the human experience, demanding a response that acknowledges both the futility and the freedom inherent in this confrontation.

Rejection of Traditional Metaphysics: Camus's philosophy rejects traditional metaphysical or religious claims that seek to provide transcendent meaning. Instead, he argues that life's inherent meaninglessness should not lead to despair or resignation but should be embraced as a starting point for constructing personal significance. By accepting that there are no ultimate answers or divine purposes, individuals can focus on creating their own meaning through lived experiences and personal choices (Camus, The Plague, 1947). This stance is both a critique of traditional belief systems and a call to action: rather than seeking solace in metaphysical assurances, individuals are invited to engage with life directly and meaningfully.

Revolt as a Response: Central to Camus's philosophy is the concept of "revolt"—a conscious and deliberate choice to live with the awareness of the absurd without succumbing to despair or nihilism. This revolt is not about rebellion against a deity or cosmic order but about asserting one's agency and finding fulfillment within an indifferent universe. Camus argues that this rebellion against the absurd is itself a form of dignity and freedom, allowing individuals to live authentically and passionately despite the lack of intrinsic purpose (Camus, The Myth of Sisyphus, 1942). The revolt embodies a form of existential resilience, a refusal to be defeated by the realization of life's inherent lack of meaning. It is an embrace of the human condition's rawness and a commitment to living fully in the face of it.

Practical Implications: Living without appeal to higher meaning involves practical and emotional adjustments.

Individuals must confront their existential freedom, making choices that reflect their values and desires rather than conforming to preordained narratives or expectations. This approach fosters a sense of personal responsibility and authenticity, encouraging individuals to engage with life's challenges and opportunities with clarity and intent. By acknowledging the absence of intrinsic purpose, individuals can create their own frameworks for understanding and valuing their experiences, relationships, and contributions.

Existential Empowerment: Camus's philosophy offers a form of existential empowerment. The acceptance of the absurd and the subsequent revolt against it empower individuals to forge their own paths and define their own purposes. Rather than seeking external validation or transcendence, individuals are encouraged to embrace the freedom and responsibility of shaping their own lives. This empowerment is both a personal and collective endeavor, as individuals work to build meaningful connections and create value within the bounds of their existence.

2. PRACTICAL IMPLICATIONS OF EMBRACING THE ABSURD IN DAILY LIFE

Embracing the absurd, as articulated by Albert Camus, has significant practical implications for how individuals approach their lives, relationships, and personal goals. Camus's philosophy offers a framework for living meaningfully despite the absence of intrinsic purpose, influencing daily choices and interactions in profound ways.

Living with Authenticity: Embracing the absurd involves living authentically and fully in the present moment. This means engaging with life's experiences and challenges directly, without expecting ultimate justification or cosmic validation. By focusing on personal values and immediate experiences, individuals can find satisfaction and meaning in their everyday activities and relationships. This approach encourages people to pursue their passions, engage in creative endeavors, and build meaningful connections with others based on shared experiences and mutual understanding (Camus, The Myth of Sisyphus, 1942). Living authentically requires a rejection of superficiality and a commitment to genuine self-expression, fostering deeper relationships and a more fulfilling life.

Acceptance of Life's Challenges: Embracing the absurd also involves accepting life's inherent struggles and uncertainties. Instead of seeking escape through illusions or distractions, individuals can confront difficulties head-on and find resilience through their own actions and choices. Camus uses the metaphor of Sisyphus, condemned to push a boulder up a hill for eternity, to illustrate that, even in the face of seemingly futile tasks, one can find purpose and satisfaction by embracing the struggle itself. This acceptance fosters a sense of personal empowerment and agency, allowing individuals to navigate life's challenges with a greater sense of inner strength and determination (Camus, The Myth of Sisyphus, 1942). By accepting the inevitability of struggle, individuals can cultivate a mindset of perseverance and resilience, transforming adversity into an opportunity for personal growth and self-discovery.

Creating Personal Meaning: Without the expectation of external validation or cosmic significance, individuals are free to create their own meaning through their actions and relationships. This personal meaning can be derived from various sources, including personal achievements, creative expression, acts of kindness, and contributions to the well-being of others. By focusing on what matters to them personally, individuals can cultivate a sense of purpose and fulfillment that is grounded in their own values and experiences (Camus, The Myth of Sisyphus, 1942). This process of meaning-making is inherently subjective, allowing each person to define their own sense of purpose and significance through their unique passions and contributions.

Engaging in the Present: Embracing the absurd encourages focusing on the present moment and the immediacy of human experience. By letting go of the need for ultimate answers or long-term guarantees, individuals can fully immerse themselves in the present and find joy and meaning in their immediate surroundings and interactions. This approach promotes mindfulness and appreciation for the richness of everyday life, highlighting the importance of living fully and attentively in the here and now (Camus, The Fall, 1956).

Practical Applications

Personal Relationships: In personal relationships, embracing the absurd can lead to deeper and more authentic connections. By focusing on the present and valuing shared experiences, individuals can build stronger bonds and foster more meaningful interactions with others. This approach encourages openness, vulnerability, and genuine communication, enhancing the quality of relationships.

Work and Creativity: In professional and creative pursuits, embracing the absurd can inspire individuals to pursue their passions with greater dedication and joy. By rejecting the need for ultimate validation and focusing on the intrinsic value of their work, individuals can find satisfaction and fulfillment in their efforts. This mindset encourages innovation and resilience in the face of challenges.

Personal Growth: Embracing the absurd fosters a proactive approach to personal growth. By accepting life's uncertainties and focusing on personal values, individuals can set meaningful goals and strive for continuous self-improvement. This approach emphasizes personal responsibility and the importance of creating one's path.

Camus's philosophy encourages a direct engagement with life's complexities, fostering a deeper appreciation for the richness of human existence in the face of an indifferent universe. By rejecting traditional notions of transcendent purpose and embracing the absurd, individuals can find personal fulfillment through authenticity, resilience, and the creation of their own meaning.

Albert Camus's philosophy of the absurd offers a powerful and liberating framework for confronting the human condition without illusion or despair. Rather than retreating into nihilism or clinging to unfounded metaphysical assurances, Camus invites us to live fully and authentically in the face of life's inherent meaninglessness. Through the act of revolt, we affirm our freedom and embrace our responsibility to shape lives of personal significance. This existential stance empowers individuals to derive meaning from lived experience, creativity, relationships, and ethical engagement with the world—without appeal to transcendent purpose. Embracing the absurd does not diminish life's value; rather, it deepens it by urging us to live deliberately, courageously, and attentively in the here and now. In a universe that offers no ultimate answers, the act of living with integrity and intention becomes a defiant and meaningful response—one that affirms the beauty and dignity of existence itself.

CHAPTER 9
CREATING MEANING IN A MEANINGLESS WORLD

1. ROLE OF PERSONAL CREATIVITY AND INDIVIDUAL AGENCY

THEY ARE crucial tools for crafting meaning and purpose in a world perceived as inherently meaningless. By leveraging these elements, individuals can navigate the void left by the absence of inherent cosmic significance and forge a life of personal fulfillment.

Personal Creativity: Creativity allows individuals to express themselves and engage with the world in ways that reflect their unique perspectives and values. Through creative endeavors, whether in art, music, writing, or other forms of self-expression, people can find joy, explore their identities, and communicate their experiences. Creativity serves as an outlet for personal expression and enables individuals to build connections with others by sharing their unique contributions. The act of creating something meaningful can provide a sense of accomplishment and purpose, even in the absence of external validation. This creative process can transform personal experiences into something tangible, fostering a sense of agency and identity. Moreover, creativity can act as a form of resilience, helping individuals cope with life's challenges and uncertainties by providing a constructive outlet for their emotions and thoughts (Kaufman, The Psychology of Creativity, 2009).

Individual Agency: Agency refers to the capacity of individuals to act independently and make choices that align with their values and goals. By exercising agency, individuals can take ownership of their lives and shape their experiences according to their preferences and aspirations. This sense of control and responsibility empowers people to pursue their own paths, set meaningful goals, and make decisions that reflect their core beliefs and desires. Embracing individual agency involves recognizing that, despite the lack of intrinsic purpose in the universe, individuals have the power to create their own sources of significance. This perspective encourages proactive engagement with one's life, where decisions are made not in search of cosmic approval but in alignment with personal values and passions. By taking deliberate actions, individuals can craft a narrative of their own lives that provides a sense of coherence and purpose (Bandura, Agentic Perspective, 2006).

Intersection of Creativity and Agency: The interplay between personal creativity and individual agency offers a dynamic approach to constructing meaning. Creativity can inform and enrich personal agency, providing new ways to interpret and respond to life's challenges. Conversely, exercising agency allows individuals to channel their creative impulses into actionable projects and goals. This synergy can lead to a more profound sense of fulfillment as individuals create and navigate their paths with intentionality and passion. By integrating creativity into their daily lives and exercising their capacity for choice, individuals can cultivate a life of richness and meaning, even within a context that lacks inherent cosmic significance.

Practical Applications: Embracing personal creativity and agency has practical implications for various aspects of life. In professional contexts, creativity can drive innovation and problem-solving, while agency enables individuals to pursue careers that align with their values and interests. In personal relationships, creativity fosters connection through shared experiences and expressions, while agency empowers individuals to shape their relationships in ways that reflect their desires and boundaries. In personal growth, creativity and agency together support the pursuit of self-improvement and personal goals, contributing to a fulfilling and self-directed life.

Challenges and Considerations: Personal creativity and individual agency play a vital role in constructing meaning and purpose in a universe that offers no inherent cosmic significance. Through creative expression and deliberate action, individuals can forge paths of personal fulfillment and navigate life's complexities with resilience and intention. However, this process is not without its challenges. The pressure to create a meaningful life or to achieve personal significance can sometimes lead to feelings of inadequacy or self-doubt. Exercising agency requires courage, as individuals must confront uncertainty, face potential setbacks, and sustain themselves through periods of ambiguity. For this reason, it is essential to balance aspirations with self-compassion and realistic expectations—recognizing that the journey of meaning-making is itself valuable, regardless of specific outcomes.

2. STRATEGIES FOR FINDING OR CREATING SIGNIFICANCE IN LIFE

Creating meaning in a seemingly indifferent world involves actively engaging with various strategies to discover and cultivate personal significance. These strategies can range from setting and pursuing goals to building meaningful relationships and contributing to the greater good.

Setting Personal Goals: One effective strategy for creating meaning is to set and pursue personal goals that align with one's values and passions. Goals provide direction and purpose, helping individuals focus their efforts and measure their progress. Whether the goals are related to career achievements, personal growth, or hobbies, they offer a sense of accomplishment and fulfillment. The process of setting and striving toward goals also fosters a sense of purpose and motivation, as individuals see their efforts leading to tangible outcomes. Goal-setting encourages individuals to envision their future, develop actionable plans, and overcome obstacles—contributing to a heightened sense of achievement and personal fulfillment (Locke & Latham, A Theory of Goal Setting and Task Performance, 1990).

Cultivating Relationships: Building and nurturing meaningful relationships with others is another critical strategy for creating significance. Human connections provide emotional support, shared experiences, and a sense of belonging. Engaging in supportive and fulfilling relationships can enhance one's sense of purpose and overall well-being. Relationships offer opportunities for mutual growth, collaboration, and shared goals, enriching one's life and providing a context for personal meaning. By investing time and effort into meaningful relationships, individuals can cultivate deeper bonds that foster a sense of interconnectedness and emotional support—factors that, in turn, reinforce their own sense of significance and belonging (Baumeister & Leary, The Need to Belong: Desire for Interpersonal Attachments as a Fundamental Human Motivation, 1995).

Contributing to Others: Contributing to the well-being of others and engaging in acts of kindness and service can also foster a sense of meaning. By making a positive impact on the lives of others, individuals can experience a sense of purpose and fulfillment. This contribution can take many forms, including volunteer work, mentoring, or supporting causes that align with personal values. Helping others benefits those who receive support and reinforces the giver's sense of significance and connection to a larger community. Engaging in altruistic activities can foster a sense of accomplishment and life satisfaction, while also enhancing well-being by promoting feelings of belonging and contributing to a greater good (Seligman, Flourish: A Visionary New Understanding of Happiness and Well-Being, 2011).

Pursuing Personal Passions: Engaging in activities and pursuits that resonate deeply with one's interests and passions can be a powerful way to find meaning. Personal passions, whether related to creative pursuits, intellectual interests, or recreational activities, provide a source of joy and satisfaction. By dedicating time and energy to these activities, individuals can create a sense of purpose and fulfillment that enriches their lives and reflects their authentic selves. Pursuing personal passions can cultivate a state of flow, in which individuals become fully immersed in their activities, experiencing deep engagement, fulfillment, and contentment (Csikszentmihalyi, Flow: The Psychology of Optimal Experience, 1990).

Embracing Mindfulness and Presence: Mindfulness and presence involve focusing on the here and now, appreciating the current moment, and finding meaning in everyday experiences. Practicing mindfulness can help individuals become more aware of their thoughts, feelings, and surroundings, fostering a deeper connection to their immediate experiences. By embracing the present moment, individuals can find significance in the superficial aspects of life and cultivate a sense of gratitude and contentment. Mindfulness encourages individuals to fully engage with their present experiences, helping to reduce stress and enhance overall well-being by fostering a more balanced, accepting, and appreciative outlook (Kabat-Zinn, Wherever You Go, There You Are: Mindfulness Meditation in Everyday Life, 1994).

Exploring Spirituality and Personal Beliefs: While not necessarily religious, exploring spirituality or personal beliefs can also provide a framework for finding meaning. This exploration might involve reflecting on personal values, engaging in practices that resonate with one's sense of purpose, or seeking out philosophical or spiritual communities that align with one's outlook on life. By contemplating and integrating personal beliefs or spiritual practices, individuals can create a sense of coherence and purpose that resonates with their inner convictions and contributes to their overall sense of meaning.

Engaging in Continuous Learning and Growth: Lifelong learning and personal development offer opportunities to explore new interests, acquire new skills, and expand one's understanding of the world. By actively seeking out new experiences and challenges, individuals can foster a sense of growth and discovery. Continuous learning encourages curiosity and adaptability, helping individuals stay engaged and motivated as they navigate their personal and professional lives. This approach not only contributes to personal fulfillment but also enriches one's perspective and sense of purpose.

Finding Joy in Simple Pleasures: Sometimes, meaning can be found in the everyday moments and simple pleasures of life. By paying attention to and appreciating small joys— such as a beautiful sunset, a warm cup of coffee, or a meaningful conversation—individuals can cultivate a sense of gratitude and contentment. Recognizing and savoring these moments can contribute to a deeper appreciation for life and reinforce a sense of significance within the context of daily experiences.

To summarize, creating meaning in a seemingly indifferent world involves harnessing personal creativity and individual agency to forge a fulfilling and purposeful life. The strategies in this chapter offer diverse pathways to discover and nurture personal meaning, enabling individuals to craft a life rich in purpose and satisfaction, grounded in personal values and experiences.

CHAPTER 10
PHILOSOPHICAL AND SCIENTIFIC RECONCILIATION

1. INTEGRATING PHILOSOPHICAL AND SCIENTIFIC PERSPECTIVES ON MEANINGLESSNESS

PHILOSOPHICAL AND SCIENTIFIC perspectives often approach the concept of "meaninglessness" from different angles, each providing valuable insights into the human experience. Integrating these viewpoints can offer a more nuanced understanding of meaninglessness and suggest ways individuals might navigate it.

Philosophical Perspectives

Philosophy delves deeply into existential questions surrounding meaning, purpose, and human existence. Existentialists, like Albert Camus and Jean-Paul Sartre, contend with the nature of the absurd and the pursuit of personal meaning in a universe that seems indifferent to human concerns.

Albert Camus: As discussed before, Camus's philosophy revolves around the conflict between humanity's inherent desire for meaning and the universe's indifferent silence. He advocates for a form of rebellion against the absurd, where individuals assert their meaning through authentic living and personal fulfillment (Camus, The Myth of Sisyphus, 1942).

Jean-Paul Sartre: For Sartre, individuals must confront the "nothingness" at the heart of existence and forge their path, making choices that reflect their authentic selves. This existential freedom allows individuals to define their essence through their actions and decisions (Sartre, Being and Nothingness, 1943).

Scientific Perspectives

Science provides empirical insights into the nature of existence and the structure of the universe, offering a different dimension to the understanding of "meaninglessness."

Evolutionary Biology: Darwin's work emphasizes the randomness and adaptiveness of evolutionary processes, which contribute to the complexity of life without implying any intrinsic purpose or purpose (Darwin, On the Origin of Species, 1859).

Cosmology: Richard Dawkins's concept of the "selfish gene" further explains how biological complexity and behavior are driven by genetic imperatives rather than any cosmic purpose. This scientific perspective highlights the absence of an overarching purpose but often lacks a focus on the subjective experiences of meaninglessness (Dawkins, The Selfish Gene, 1976).

Reconciling Perspectives

Integrating philosophical and scientific perspectives involves acknowledging the strengths and limitations of each viewpoint and finding ways in which they can complement one another.

Philosophy and Science in Dialogue: While science describes the mechanisms underlying existence, philosophy addresses the subjective implications of these findings. For example, scientific explanations of the universe's vastness and life's evolutionary processes offer a backdrop against which philosophical inquiry can explore the implications for human meaning and purpose. This integration enables a more holistic understanding of human experience—one that incorporates both empirical evidence and existential reflection (Nagel, The View from Nowhere, 1986; Wilson, Consilience, 1998).

Empirical Evidence and Existential Reflection: Recognizing that scientific insights reveal the mechanisms and structures of existence, at the same time, philosophical inquiry addresses the human response to these revelations, which can lead to a richer understanding of meaninglessness. This approach fosters a comprehensive view that considers both the objective aspects of existence and the subjective experiences of individuals grappling with meaning.

Integrating philosophical and scientific perspectives on meaninglessness provides a multifaceted understanding of human existence. Philosophy offers insights into personal and subjective responses to the absence of intrinsic purpose, while science explains the empirical realities of existence. Combining these approaches enriches our understanding and helps us navigate the challenges of meaninglessness in a complex world.

2. HOW A MULTIDISCIPLINARY APPROACH CAN ENRICH OUR UNDERSTANDING

A multidisciplinary approach, combining philosophical, scientific, psychological, and sociological perspectives, offers a more comprehensive and nuanced understanding of meaninglessness and the quest for significance. Each discipline contributes unique insights, enriching our grasp of these complex issues.

Philosophical Enrichment

Philosophy provides a foundational framework for exploring existential questions, ethics, and human experience. By integrating philosophical insights with scientific findings, individuals gain a deeper, contextual understanding of existential issues.

Existential Philosophy and Science: Philosophical reflections on meaning can be enhanced by scientific insights into the universe's scale and the processes of evolution. For example, Camus's concept of the absurd gains additional depth when viewed alongside scientific discoveries about the vastness of the cosmos and the randomness of evolutionary processes (Camus, The Myth of Sisyphus, 1942; Sartre, Being and Nothingness, 1943).

Ethical Reflections and Empirical Data: Philosophy also explores ethical dimensions and the nature of human values. By integrating ethical theories with empirical data from scientific research, individuals can better understand how moral and ethical frameworks are influenced by biological, psychological, and social factors. This approach can offer a more rounded view of how people make meaning in their lives and the role of ethical considerations in their pursuit of significance.

Scientific Enrichment

Science contributes empirical data and theories that inform our understanding of the natural world and human existence. Integrating scientific perspectives with philosophical inquiry leads to a more nuanced comprehension of how natural processes affect human life and consciousness.

Cognitive Science and Philosophy: Insights from cognitive

science and neuroscience offer valuable perspectives on the workings of the brain, consciousness, and selfhood. These scientific findings can inform and enrich philosophical discourse on the nature of mind and identity. For instance, understanding the neurological underpinnings of subjective experience contributes to deeper philosophical debates about the nature of the self and personal continuity (Damasio, Descartes' Error, 1994; Pinker, The Blank Slate, 2002).

Evolutionary Biology and Human Behavior: Evolutionary biology offers explanations for human behavior and values based on natural selection and genetic inheritance. Integrating these explanations with philosophical and psychological insights can help elucidate how evolutionary processes shape human experiences, including our search for meaning. This interdisciplinary approach can show how biological imperatives influence our values and sense of purpose (Dawkins, The Selfish Gene, 1976).

Psychological and Sociological Perspectives

Psychological and sociological perspectives provide additional layers of understanding by examining how individuals and societies cope with existential concerns and construct meaning.

Psychological Approaches to Meaning: Psychology explores how individuals manage existential anxiety and find personal meaning. Techniques such as cognitive-behavioral therapy and mindfulness can offer practical strategies for dealing with feelings of meaninglessness. Integrating psychological approaches with philosophical reflection can equip individuals with practical tools for cultivating personal significance and meaning (Frankl, Man's Search for Meaning, 1946; Csikszentmihalyi, Flow, 1990).

Sociological Contexts and Meaning: Sociology examines how cultural, social, and historical contexts shape human values and beliefs. By understanding how societal factors influence the construction of meaning, individuals can gain insights into how different cultures and communities approach existential questions. This sociological perspective can complement philosophical and scientific insights, offering a broader view of how meaning is constructed across various contexts (Durkheim, The Elementary Forms of Religious Life, 1912).

Practical Applications

A multidisciplinary approach has practical implications for addressing meaninglessness in everyday life. By combining philosophical reflections with practical psychological strategies and scientific knowledge, individuals can develop more effective methods for navigating existential challenges.

Personal Fulfillment: Integrating philosophical insights on personal meaning with psychological techniques for coping with existential anxiety can provide individuals with a comprehensive toolkit for finding purpose and satisfaction in their lives.

Informed Decision-Making: Combining scientific knowledge about human biology and behavior with philosophical insights can aid individuals in making decisions that align with their values and goals. This approach fosters a deeper understanding of how to live a fulfilling and meaningful life, grounded in both empirical evidence and existential reflection.

Reconciling philosophical and scientific perspectives on meaninglessness involves integrating insights from both domains to offer a more comprehensive understanding of human existence. By merging empirical evidence with existential reflection, individuals can gain a deeper appreciation of the complexities of existence and develop nuanced strategies for creating and navigating personal meaning in a seemingly indifferent universe. This comprehensive framework enhances our ability to address fundamental questions of existence and effectively navigate the challenges of finding significance in a complex world.

The reconciliation of philosophical and scientific perspectives on meaninglessness offers a powerful, multidimensional framework for understanding the human condition. Where science elucidates the mechanics of existence and the indifferent nature of the cosmos, philosophy explores the existential implications of this reality and the ways individuals respond to it. By integrating these approaches—along with insights from psychology and sociology—we gain a more holistic comprehension of how meaning is constructed, challenged, and redefined across personal and cultural contexts. This multidisciplinary synergy enables us not only to grasp the nature of our existential predicament but also to cultivate strategies for living purposefully in its midst. Rather than viewing meaninglessness as a void, this approach reframes it as a space for creative, ethical, and authentic engagement with life. In doing so, it empowers individuals to forge their own sense of meaning through reflective action, emotional resilience, and intellectual clarity—anchored not in cosmic assurances, but in the richness of human thought and experience.

CHAPTER 11
ETHICAL IMPLICATIONS AND HUMAN FLOURISHING

1. ETHICAL CONSIDERATIONS IN A SEEMINGLY INDIFFERENT UNIVERSE

IN A UNIVERSE that appears indifferent to human concerns, ethical considerations take on a unique significance. The apparent absence of intrinsic purpose or purpose in the cosmos challenges traditional moral frameworks and raises important questions about how individuals should act and live ethically.

Moral Relativism and Absolutism: In the face of the universe's indifference, moral relativism and absolutism offer differing perspectives on ethics. Moral relativism suggests that ethical principles are not universal but are instead shaped by cultural, social, or individual contexts. This view implies that, in the absence of objective meaning, ethical values are constructed rather than discovered (Harman, Moral Relativism and Moral Objectivity, 1996).

In contrast, moral absolutism suggests that certain moral principles are universally valid and apply regardless of the context. Absolutists argue that even in an indifferent universe, ethical norms can provide a sense of direction and coherence (Kant, Groundwork of the Metaphysics of Morals, 1785). This perspective suggests that certain fundamental moral truths persist despite the lack of inherent cosmic meaning.

Existentialist Ethics: Existentialist philosophy provides its own approach to ethics in the context of meaninglessness. Existentialists such as Jean-Paul Sartre and Simone de Beauvoir argue that individuals must create their own values and ethical frameworks through authentic engagement with their freedom and responsibility (Sartre, Existentialism Is a Humanism, 1946; de Beauvoir, The Second Sex, 1949).

This perspective emphasizes personal responsibility and the importance of acting in a way that reflects one's chosen values. In an indifferent universe, existentialist ethics suggest that individuals must confront their freedom to make choices and bear the consequences, thus creating meaning through their actions and commitments.

Ethical Naturalism: Ethical naturalism holds that moral values can be grounded in our understanding of human nature and the natural world. This perspective integrates scientific insights into human behavior and well-being to construct ethical frameworks that align with our evolutionary traits and social needs (Wilson, The Social Conquest of Earth, 2012). Ethical naturalism aims to ground moral principles in empirical observations about human flourishing and social cooperation. By understanding human nature and the conditions that promote well-being, ethical naturalism provides a way to establish ethics that are practical and relevant, even in a seemingly indifferent universe.

Pragmatic Ethics: Pragmatic ethics focuses on the practical

consequences of ethical decisions and the utility of moral principles in fostering human well-being and social harmony. This approach evaluates ethical theories based on their ability to address real-world problems and improve human life. In a universe lacking intrinsic purpose, pragmatic ethics suggests that ethical standards should be judged by their effectiveness in promoting human flourishing, reducing suffering, and facilitating cooperation (Dewey, The Public and Its Problems, 1927).

Humanistic Ethics: Humanistic ethics centers on the intrinsic value of human beings and their capacity for reason, empathy, and moral judgment. This perspective emphasizes the importance of respecting human dignity and promoting individual and collective well-being. In the face of the universe's indifference, humanistic ethics argues that moral principles should be grounded in the recognition of human worth and the pursuit of a more just and compassionate society (Maslow, Motivation and Personality, 1954). By focusing on the inherent qualities of humanity and the potential for positive social change, humanistic ethics provides a framework for ethical behavior that aligns with our shared values and aspirations.

2. PERSPECTIVES ON HUMAN FLOURISHING AND WELL-BEING DESPITE EXISTENTIAL DOUBTS

Even in a universe that appears devoid of intrinsic purpose, human flourishing and well-being remain attainable through various approaches that address existential doubts and emphasize personal growth. These perspectives offer strategies for cultivating a fulfilling and meaningful life despite the absence of cosmic significance.

Humanistic Psychology: Humanistic psychology, pioneered by figures such as Abraham Maslow, emphasizes self-actualization and personal growth as central to human flourishing. Maslow's hierarchy of needs culminates in self-actualization, which involves realizing one's full potential and achieving personal fulfillment through creative expression and meaningful pursuits (Maslow, Motivation and Personality, 1954). This approach highlights that, even in the face of existential doubts, individuals can find purpose and satisfaction by focusing on their intrinsic goals, personal development, and self-expression.

Positive Psychology: Positive psychology, developed by Martin Seligman, focuses on the study and promotion of positive emotions, strengths, and virtues that contribute to human well-being. Seligman's work emphasizes the cultivation of a life filled with meaningful goals, gratitude, and resilience (Seligman, Authentic Happiness, 2002).

Positive psychology offers practical strategies for enhancing life satisfaction, such as engaging in activities that bring joy, practicing gratitude, and building strong social connections.

Eudaimonia and Virtue Ethics: Eudaimonia, a concept rooted in Aristotelian virtue ethics, suggests that human flourishing is achieved through the cultivation of moral virtues and the pursuit of a virtuous life. Aristotle defines eudaimonia as the highest form of human good, attained by living in accordance with virtues such as courage, temperance, and wisdom (Aristotle, Nicomachean Ethics, 350 BCE). This perspective emphasizes that aligning one's actions with ethical principles and contributing to both personal and communal well-being can lead to a meaningful and fulfilling life, even in a seemingly indifferent universe.

Existential Fulfillment: Existential psychology, notably advanced by Viktor Frankl, suggests that individuals can find fulfillment by pursuing personal meaning and purpose despite existential doubts. Frankl's concept of "logotherapy" centers on the search for meaning as a core aspect of human existence, advocating that individuals achieve well-being by identifying and pursuing meaningful goals and values (Frankl, Man's Search for Meaning, 1946). This approach underscores the importance of personal agency and the capacity to create significance in one's life, reinforcing that fulfillment can be found through the active pursuit of meaningful endeavors.

Mindfulness and Acceptance: Mindfulness and acceptance practices offer valuable tools for coping with existential doubts and enhancing well-being. Rooted in various philosophical and psychological traditions, these practices involve cultivating awareness of the present moment and embracing life's uncertainties (Kabat-Zinn, Wherever You Go, There You Are, 1994). By focusing on the present and accepting the inherent ambiguity of existence, individuals can foster a sense of peace and resilience. Mindfulness practices help individuals to engage fully with their experiences, reduce stress, and build a more balanced and contented approach to life.

Existential Positive Psychology: A synthesis of existential and positive psychology approaches focuses on finding meaning through the pursuit of personal strengths and values. This perspective integrates existential concerns with positive psychological practices, encouraging individuals to identify and engage with their core values and passions. By doing so, individuals can create a fulfilling and purposeful life that aligns with their authentic selves while addressing existential questions about the nature of existence (Seligman, Flourish, 2011; Yalom, Existential Psychotherapy, 1980).

In summary, navigating existential doubts and finding fulfillment in a seemingly indifferent universe involves exploring a range of ethical frameworks and perspectives on human flourishing. While traditional moral frameworks might be challenged by the universe's indifference, approaches like existentialist ethics and ethical naturalism provide ways to address ethical dilemmas.

PART FOUR
REFLECTIONS AND FURTHER QUESTIONS

CHAPTER 12
THE FUTURE OF EXISTENTIAL INQUIRY

1. EMERGING TRENDS IN EXISTENTIAL PHILOSOPHY AND SCIENCE

AS WE ADVANCE into the 21st century, existential inquiry continues to evolve, influenced by emerging trends in both philosophy and science. These developments reflect an ongoing quest to understand the nature of meaning and human existence in light of contemporary challenges and new insights.

Existential Psychology and Neuroscience: Recent advancements in psychology and neuroscience are providing new perspectives on existential concerns. Existential psychology delves into how individuals grapple with issues like death anxiety, identity, and the search for meaning. This field is increasingly integrating findings from neuroscience to understand how brain processes are linked to existential experiences. For instance, neuroimaging studies are exploring correlations between brain activity and experiences of existential anxiety and personal meaning-making (Yalom, Existential Psychotherapy, 1980). This interdisciplinary approach aims to bridge the gap between subjective existential experiences and objective neurological data, offering a more comprehensive understanding of how existential issues manifest in the brain and affect behavior.

Philosophy of Technology and Artificial Intelligence: The rapid advancement of technology, particularly artificial intelligence (AI), is prompting new existential questions. Philosophers are examining the implications of AI for human identity, autonomy, and the nature of meaning (Bostrom, Superintelligence: Paths, Dangers, Strategies, 2014). Issues such as AI's impact on employment, privacy, and ethical decision-making are raising fundamental questions about human purpose and the role of technology in shaping our lives.

The development of AI also challenges traditional notions of consciousness and agency, leading to debates about what it means to be human in a world where machines might replicate or even surpass human cognitive abilities.

Ecopsychology and Environmental Existentialism: The environmental crisis and climate change have spurred the growth of ecopsychology and ecological existentialism, fields that explore the connection between human psychology and the natural environment. Ecopsychology examines how ecological concerns influence existential reflections and the search for meaning, highlighting the psychological impact of environmental destruction (Roszak, The Voice of the Earth, 1992). Environmental existentialism considers how awareness of ecological degradation affects our sense of purpose and responsibility, emphasizing the need for a deeper connection to the natural world.

Transhumanism and the Quest for Immortality: Transhumanism is a movement focused on enhancing human capabilities through technology and extending life through scientific advancements. This trend raises profound existential questions about the nature of humanity, the desire for immortality, and the search for meaning in an era where traditional boundaries of life and death are increasingly challenged (Kurzweil, The Singularity Is Near, 2005). Philosophers and scientists are exploring how these technological advancements impact our understanding of existence and purpose, considering whether the pursuit of radical life extension and cognitive enhancement might alter fundamental aspects of what it means to be human.

By integrating insights from psychology, technology, environmental studies, and transhumanism, we gain a richer and more nuanced understanding of existential questions and the search for meaning in a rapidly changing world.

2. HOW CONTEMPORARY THINKERS ARE ADDRESSING THE QUESTION OF MEANING

Contemporary philosophers and scholars are developing innovative approaches to address existential questions and the search for meaning in today's complex world. These approaches reflect diverse perspectives and seek to integrate traditional existential concerns with modern challenges.

Postmodern Existentialism: Postmodern existentialism critiques traditional narratives and explores how meaning is constructed in a fragmented and diverse world. Thinkers like Jean-François Lyotard and Michel Foucault delve into how meaning is shaped by language, power structures, and cultural narratives (Lyotard, The Postmodern Condition, 1979; Foucault, Discipline and Punish, 1975). This perspective highlights the fluid and contingent nature of meaning, suggesting that individuals must actively navigate and construct their significance amidst a plurality of conflicting narratives and values. Postmodern existentialism challenges the notion of universal truths, emphasizing the importance of personal and cultural context in the search for meaning.

Integrative Existentialism: Integrative existentialism seeks to synthesize insights from existential philosophy with other disciplines, such as psychology, sociology, and theology. This approach aims to develop a more comprehensive understanding of meaning by drawing on diverse sources of wisdom and experience. For example, Viktor Frankl's logotherapy combines existential concerns with psychological practice, offering tools for finding meaning through personal values and goals (Frankl, Man's Search for Meaning, 1946). Contemporary integrative existentialists extend this approach by incorporating findings from modern science and cultural studies, seeking to create a holistic framework that addresses both individual and societal dimensions of meaning.

Interfaith and Intercultural Perspectives: In an increasingly globalized world, intercultural and interfaith dialogue are crucial for exploring existential questions. Scholars are investigating how various religious and cultural traditions approach meaning and purpose, aiming to find common ground and foster mutual understanding (Armstrong, The Case for God, 2009). This approach values diverse perspectives and promotes a more inclusive and empathetic exploration of existential concerns. By engaging with multiple traditions and cultural contexts, contemporary thinkers seek to enrich our understanding of meaning and purpose across different belief systems and practices.

Existential Social Justice: Existential social justice explores the intersection of existential philosophy with social justice issues. This perspective examines how questions of meaning and purpose relate to systemic inequalities, oppression, and human rights (Young, Justice and the Politics of Difference, 1990). It emphasizes the importance of addressing social injustices in the search for individual and collective meaning. By linking existential concerns with activism and advocacy, existential social justice highlights the role of ethical action and social responsibility in creating a meaningful life.

Digital Existentialism: The rise of digital technology and social media creates new existential questions about identity, community, and meaning. Digital existentialism examines how virtual environments impact our sense of self and our interactions with others. Scholars explore how online identities, and digital interactions shape our existential experiences and contribute to or undermine our search for meaning (Turkle, Alone Together: Why We Expect More from Technology and Less from Each Other, 2011). This emerging field seeks to understand the implications of digital life for personal and collective significance, addressing how technology both complicates and enriches our existential inquiries.

The future of existential inquiry is marked by emerging trends that reflect new scientific discoveries, technological advancements, and evolving philosophical perspectives. The approaches in this chapter address the enduring question of meaning in a rapidly changing world, offering diverse and innovative ways to understand and navigate the complexities of human existence.

As existential inquiry moves forward, it continues to adapt to the dynamic contours of the modern world, integrating new insights from science, technology, culture, and philosophy. The convergence of disciplines—from neuroscience and AI ethics to ecopsychology and digital identity—demonstrates that the search for meaning is no longer confined to traditional philosophical boundaries.

Instead, it is an ever-expanding dialogue that reflects humanity's evolving challenges, aspirations, and anxieties. Contemporary thinkers are not only reexamining timeless existential themes but also reshaping them to address pressing issues such as environmental collapse, technological disruption, and social injustice. This future-oriented, multidisciplinary engagement signals that existential inquiry remains a vital, adaptive, and deeply human endeavor. By embracing complexity and diversity, it encourages individuals and societies alike to confront the unknown with curiosity, courage, and a renewed commitment to forging meaning in an uncertain world.

CHAPTER 13
THE ROLE OF ART, LITERATURE, AND CULTURE

1. EXPLORING HOW ART AND CULTURE RESPOND TO EXISTENTIAL QUESTIONS

ART AND CULTURE have historically been potent responses to existential questions, providing avenues for individuals to explore and express the complexities of meaning, purpose, and human existence. Creative expression offers unique insights into the human condition through various forms and genres, reflecting and shaping our understanding of existential issues.

Art as a Reflection of Existential Anxiety: Art often mirrors the existential anxieties and concerns of its time. Edvard Munch's The Scream (1893) powerfully encapsulates the sense of existential dread and alienation that individuals may feel when confronting the void and grappling with the search for meaning (Munch, The Scream, 1893). This iconic painting conveys an intense emotional response to the perceived meaninglessness of existence. Similarly, Salvador Dalí's surrealist masterpiece The Persistence of Memory (1931) delves into themes of absurdity and the subconscious, symbolizing the chaotic nature of human existence and the persistent search for coherence in an indifferent universe (Dalí, The Persistence of Memory, 1931). Dalí's melting clocks and dreamlike landscapes evoke the fluidity of time and reality, underscoring the instability and perplexity inherent in the human experience.

Literature and the Exploration of Existential Themes: Literature is a rich medium for exploring existential questions, offering narrative forms that delve into themes of meaning, identity, and the human condition. Franz Kafka's The Metamorphosis (1915) addresses themes of alienation and existential crisis through the story of Gregor Samsa, who inexplicably transforms into an insect and must confront a new, absurd reality. Kafka's work powerfully illustrates the profound sense of isolation and meaninglessness that individuals may experience in an indifferent and incomprehensible world (Kafka, The Metamorphosis, 1915). Similarly, Jean-Paul Sartre's existential novel Nausea (1938) portrays characters grappling with the realization of life's inherent meaninglessness and the disorientation that follows. Sartre's protagonists confront the existential void and respond to it in ways that reflect broader philosophical concerns about freedom, responsibility, and authenticity (Sartre, Nausea, 1938).

Cultural Responses to Existential Dilemmas: Different cultures have approached existential questions through distinct artistic and philosophical traditions. Eastern philosophies such as Zen Buddhism and Taoism emphasize acceptance of the present moment and the impermanence of existence—perspectives that have profoundly shaped artistic expression and cultural values (Suzuki, Zen Mind, Beginner's Mind, 1970; Watts, The Way of Zen, 1957). Zen art, in particular, often conveys a sense of tranquility and simplicity, embodying principles of mindfulness and the ephemeral nature of life.

Western existentialism, in turn, has inspired a range of artistic expressions that grapple with themes of freedom, responsibility, and the search for meaning. For instance, the existential concerns of 20th-century Europe have influenced modernist and postmodern art movements, which explore the fragmentation and ambiguity of human experience.

Film and Media as Modern Existential Platforms: In contemporary culture, film and media serve as powerful platforms for exploring existential themes. Movies such as Ingmar Bergman's The Seventh Seal (1957) and Woody Allen's Annie Hall (1977) engage deeply with questions of death, meaning, and human connection (Bergman, The Seventh Seal, 1957; Allen, Annie Hall, 1977). Bergman's film, set during the Black Death, features a knight who plays chess with Death, reflecting deep existential concerns about mortality and the search for meaning. Allen's film, with its blend of humor and introspection, explores the complexities of relationships and existential doubts.

The rise of dystopian and science fiction genres reflects contemporary anxieties surrounding technology, identity, and the future of humanity. Films such as Blade Runner (1982) and The Matrix (1999) critically explore the implications of artificial intelligence and virtual reality on human consciousness, autonomy, and meaning. These narratives offer speculative yet profound reflections on existential concerns in an increasingly digital and posthuman world.

Performing Arts and Existential Expression: The performing arts, including theater and dance, vividly explore existential themes by embodying them on stage. Samuel Beckett's Waiting for Godot (1953), for example, underscores the absurdity and futility of human endeavors through its portrayal of characters engaged in perpetual waiting. The play delves into existential questions of time, purpose, and hope in a seemingly indifferent universe (Beckett, Waiting for Godot, 1953). Similarly, contemporary dance performances often incorporate elements of existential exploration, with choreographers using movement to convey themes of identity, transformation, and the human condition. Performances that engage with existential questions offer audiences a visceral experience of these themes, allowing for emotional and intellectual engagement with the complexities of meaning and existence.

2. IMPACT OF CREATIVE EXPRESSION ON THE SEARCH FOR MEANING

Creative expression profoundly impacts individuals' search for meaning, offering pathways for both personal exploration and collective fulfillment. Through various forms of artistic engagement, people can navigate existential questions and find deeper significance in their lives.

Artistic Creation as a Means of Personal Exploration: Engaging in artistic creation provides a powerful means for individuals to explore and articulate their existential concerns. Whether through painting, writing, or music, the creative process becomes a conduit for self-discovery, allowing individuals to confront and make sense of their fears, desires, and uncertainties. As E.H. Gombrich notes in The Story of Art (1950), art is not merely about representation, but about expression and the ongoing human effort to find meaning in experience (Gombrich, The Story of Art, 1950). For instance, creating a painting might help an individual explore their emotional responses to life's challenges, while writing poetry can offer insight into their internal struggles and aspirations.

This introspective process not only helps individuals navigate their existential questions but also allows them to articulate and understand their personal sense of meaning.

Art and the Expression of Collective Identity: Art plays a pivotal role in shaping and expressing collective identity and values. Cultural artifacts such as literature, music, and visual art reflect and influence societal attitudes toward existential questions, including purpose, justice, and belonging. For instance, the Harlem Renaissance of the early 20th century generated a rich body of literary and artistic works that grappled with themes of racial identity, social struggle, and cultural aspiration. Writers such as Langston Hughes in The Big Sea (1940) and Zora Neale Hurston in Their Eyes Were Watching God (1937) gave voice to the complexities of Black experience in America, blending personal narrative with broader existential and societal reflections. This movement provided a collective voice for African American experiences, contributing to a broader understanding of meaning within a specific cultural and historical context.

By articulating shared experiences and values, art fosters a sense of unity and collective identity while also challenging and expanding societal perspectives.

Therapeutic and Transformative Potential of Art: The therapeutic benefits of art therapy highlight its effectiveness in addressing existential concerns and promoting psychological well-being. By offering a structured and creative avenue for individuals to process trauma, explore inner experiences, and construct meaning, art therapy serves as a powerful tool for self-understanding and emotional healing (Malchiodi, The Art Therapy Sourcebook, 2006).

By engaging in artistic activities, individuals can confront and work through complex emotions, uncover personal insights, and develop coping strategies.

The transformative potential of art lies in its capacity to facilitate personal growth and healing, offering individuals a means to address existential challenges and discover a sense of purpose and connection.

Art as a Source of Inspiration and Hope: Throughout history, art has served as a source of inspiration and hope, offering new perspectives on human existence and the potential for positive change. Artistic works that explore existential themes often resonate profoundly with audiences, offering both solace and inspiration in their search for meaning and purpose (Beckett, Waiting for Godot, 1953).

The ability of art to evoke empathy, provoke thought, and challenge conventional viewpoints underscores its significance in the ongoing quest for existential understanding. For instance, the themes explored in existential literature or film can offer audiences novel insights and affirmations, encouraging them to find their paths to meaning amidst life's uncertainties.

Through these various aspects of creative expression, art and culture offer valuable resources for exploring and articulating existential questions. By providing spaces for personal reflection, expressing collective values, facilitating therapeutic processes, and inspiring hope, art plays a crucial role in helping individuals and societies navigate the complexities of meaning and existence.

Art, literature, and culture remain indispensable to the existential quest, offering dynamic spaces where the profound questions of human existence are not only examined but felt, expressed, and shared. From solitary acts of creation to collective cultural movements, artistic expression allows individuals and communities to grapple with meaning, identity, suffering, and transcendence in ways that logic and reason alone cannot capture. Across media and traditions, creative works serve as mirrors to our inner lives and the external conditions that shape them, revealing both the anguish and beauty of the human condition. In a world marked by rapid change, uncertainty, and fragmentation, the enduring power of the arts provides continuity, reflection, and a sense of possibility. As existential concerns evolve, so too will the creative responses that seek to illuminate them—ensuring that the search for meaning continues to be enriched by imagination, empathy, and the transformative potential of human creativity.

CHAPTER 14
PERSONAL REFLECTIONS AND APPLICATIONS

1. ENCOURAGING READERS TO REFLECT ON THEIR OWN SEARCH FOR MEANING

AS READERS DELVE into existential inquiry, it is vital to encourage them to engage deeply with their personal search for meaning. This chapter aims to provide tools and strategies that facilitate introspection and self-discovery, helping individuals explore their own existential questions and aspirations.

Understanding Personal Existential Questions: Begin by prompting readers to identify and articulate their own existential questions. These questions might center on their purpose in life, their values, or their responses to life's inherent challenges. Encourage them to reflect on moments of profound doubt or revelation and how these experiences have influenced their understanding of meaning. For example, individuals may ask themselves questions such as, "What gives my life purpose?" or "How can I cope with feelings of existential anxiety?" (Frankl, Man's Search for Meaning, 1946). Engaging with such reflections can offer greater clarity in one's personal search for meaning and lay the groundwork for deeper philosophical or psychological exploration.

Reflecting on Personal Values and Beliefs: Encourage readers to examine their personal values and beliefs, which often form the foundation of their sense of purpose and meaning. Invite them to reflect on how well their values align with their actions and life choices. Thought-provoking questions such as "What are the core principles that guide my life?" and "How do my values shape my decisions and relationships?" can initiate this introspective process (Sartre, Existentialism Is a Humanism, 1946). By examining their values, readers can assess whether their current life path aligns with what they truly believe is important and identify areas where adjustments might be necessary to achieve a more meaningful existence.

Exploring Life's Meaning Through Relationships and Achievements: Prompt readers to reflect on how their relationships and personal achievements contribute to their sense of meaning. Relationships with family, friends, and community can provide a profound sense of purpose, as can personal accomplishments and goals. Encourage readers to consider questions like, "How do my relationships enrich my life?" and "In what ways do my achievements reflect my personal sense of purpose?" (Sennett, The Craftsman, 2008). By evaluating the role of these elements in their lives, readers can gain insight into how they derive meaning from their interactions and achievements and how they might enhance these aspects to foster a more profound sense of fulfillment.

Engaging with Creative Expression: Suggest that readers explore creative expression as a means of self-discovery and meaning-making. Engaging in art, writing, or music can provide a valuable outlet for expressing existential concerns and exploring personal identity. Encourage them to reflect on how their creative endeavors help them process their thoughts and emotions about meaning. Questions, like "How does creating art help me understand my existential questions?" and "In what ways does my creative work reflect my search for purpose?" can guide this exploration.

Considering the Impact of External Influences: Invite readers to examine how external influences, such as societal expectations, cultural norms, and life experiences, shape their search for meaning. Encourage them to reflect on questions, like "How do societal expectations affect my sense of purpose?" and "What role do cultural norms play in shaping my values and beliefs?" By understanding the impact of these factors, readers can gain a more comprehensive view of how external influences intersect with their personal quest for meaning.

Practicing Mindfulness and Reflection: Encourage readers to incorporate mindfulness practices into their daily lives as a tool for exploring existential questions and fostering self-awareness. Mindfulness techniques, such as meditation and journaling, can help individuals become more attuned to their inner experiences and gain clarity on their sense of purpose. Suggest questions, like "How does mindfulness help me understand my own existential concerns?" and "What insights have I gained through reflective practices?" to support this exploration.

2. PRACTICAL EXERCISES AND PROMPTS FOR PERSONAL EXPLORATION

To facilitate personal exploration and help readers engage deeply with their existential concerns, this section provides practical exercises and prompts. These activities encourage self-reflection, creativity, and proactive steps toward finding meaning in their lives.

Journaling for Self-Discovery: Journaling is a powerful tool for self-reflection and can be instrumental in exploring existential questions. Encourage readers to set aside regular time for journaling about their thoughts, feelings, and experiences related to meaning and purpose. Here are some prompts to guide their reflections:

- "Describe a moment when you felt most alive and connected to your purpose. What were you doing, and how did it impact your sense of meaning?"
- "Write about a time when you confronted a significant challenge. How did this experience shape your understanding of meaning and your approach to life?"
- "Reflect on a time when you felt disconnected or lost. What factors contributed to this feeling, and what did you learn from it?"

Vision Board Creation: A vision board serves as a powerful visual representation of one's goals, values, and aspirations. Encourage readers to collect images, quotes, and symbols that reflect their deepest motivations and desired life changes. Once complete, guide them to engage in thoughtful reflection using the following prompts:

- Which images or symbols resonate with me most deeply, and why?
- How do these visual elements align with my sense of purpose and the changes I wish to make in my life?
- What does the process of creating this vision board reveal about my current priorities, values, and aspirations?

(Pennebaker, Opening Up: The Healing Power of Expressing Emotions, 1997; Norton, The Secret to an Extraordinary Life, 2009)

Mindfulness and Meditation Practices: Mindfulness and meditation can serve as powerful tools for exploring existential concerns and fostering inner clarity. Encourage readers to establish a regular mindfulness meditation practice, focusing on being fully present and observing thoughts and emotions without judgment. Reflection prompts may include:

- What thoughts or emotions arise when I reflect on the meaning of my life? How do these experiences shape my sense of purpose?
- In what ways can mindfulness help me find clarity, balance, or peace in my search for meaning?
- Think about a recent mindfulness session. What insights emerged about my personal values, fears, or aspirations?

(Kabat-Zinn, Wherever You Go, There You Are, 1994)

Creating a Personal Mission Statement: Crafting a personal mission statement can serve as a compass for your life, offering clarity, purpose, and a grounded sense of direction. Invite readers to reflect deeply on their values, passions, and long-term aspirations, and then articulate a guiding statement that captures their vision for their life. To assist in this process, consider the following prompts:

- What are my most cherished values, and how do they influence my choices and behaviors?
- What kind of legacy or impact do I hope to leave behind, and how does this reflect my inner sense of meaning?
- How can a clear personal mission statement shape both my everyday decisions and broader life goals?

(Covey, The 7 Habits of Highly Effective People, 1989)

Engaging in Creative Expression: Encourage readers to explore various forms of creative expression for self-discovery and meaning-making. This could involve activities such as painting, writing, composing music, or performing. Reflect on the role of creativity in their search for meaning with prompts such as:

- "How does engaging in creative activities help me process my existential concerns and explore my identity?"
- "What themes or emotions frequently emerge in my creative work, and what might they reveal about my search for meaning?"
- "How can I incorporate creative expression into my daily life to enhance my sense of purpose and fulfillment?"

Setting and Pursuing Personal Goals: Specific, achievable goals can help readers achieve a more meaningful and fulfilling life. Encourage them to identify short-term and long-term goals that align with their values and aspirations. Use prompts like:

- "What are three specific goals I want to achieve in the next year, and how do they align with my sense of purpose?"
- "What steps can I take to overcome obstacles and stay motivated in pursuing these goals?"

- "How will achieving these goals contribute to my overall sense of meaning and fulfillment?"

These exercises and prompts aim to facilitate a deeper exploration of personal existential concerns and support the readers of this book in finding their paths to meaning and fulfillment. By engaging in these activities, individuals can gain valuable insights, develop a clearer sense of purpose, and take actionable steps toward a more meaningful life.

Readers are encouraged to embark on a personal journey of self-reflection and exploration, providing practical tools and exercises to aid in their search for meaning. By engaging with their own existential questions, reflecting on personal values and relationships, and applying creative and mindfulness practices, readers can gain deeper insights into their purpose and fulfillment.

Ultimately, the journey toward meaning is deeply personal, shaped by each individual's experiences, values, and aspirations. This chapter has aimed to provide not only intellectual guidance but also practical tools that empower readers to actively engage in their own existential exploration. Whether through journaling, mindfulness, creative expression, or intentional goal-setting, the pursuit of meaning becomes a lived process— one that evolves through reflection, discovery, and transformation. By embracing this journey with openness and courage, readers can cultivate a life that is more aligned with their authentic selves, enriched by purpose, and resilient in the face of life's uncertainties. In doing so, they not only find meaning for themselves but also contribute meaningfully to the lives of others and to the broader human story.

CONCLUSION: THE JOURNEY CONTINUES

1. SUMMARY OF KEY INSIGHTS AND PERSPECTIVES FROM THE BOOK

As we reach the conclusion of our exploration into existential inquiry, it is valuable to consolidate the key insights and perspectives covered throughout the book. Each chapter has contributed to a nuanced understanding of the search for meaning in a seemingly indifferent universe, drawing from diverse fields, including philosophy, science, and art.

Nature of the Absurd: We started with Albert Camus's concept of the absurd, highlighting the conflict between humanity's intrinsic quest for meaning and the universe's inherent indifference. Camus's exploration of this fundamental discrepancy challenges us to confront the lack of intrinsic purpose. It encourages us to find ways to live authentically despite it (Camus, The Myth of Sisyphus, 1942). This idea suggests that, while the universe may be indifferent, individuals can create personal significance by responding to the absurd.

Schopenhauer's Pessimism and the Will to Live: Arthur Schopenhauer's philosophy introduced the notion of the Will as a fundamental driving force behind human suffering and striving. Schopenhauer's pessimistic view of life's inherent meaninglessness and the perpetual striving of the Will underscores the existential struggle accompanying our quest for purpose (Schopenhauer, The

World as Will and Representation, 1818). His perspective illuminates the relentless nature of human desire and the challenges it poses for finding contentment and meaning.

Nietzsche's Nihilism and the Übermensch: Friedrich Nietzsche's critique of traditional values and his concept of nihilism, symbolized by the "death of God," catalyzed existential questioning. Nietzsche proposed the Übermensch (Overman) as a solution to the void left by the collapse of absolute truths. He encouraged the creation of personal values and meaning, advocating for a proactive approach to forging one's purpose without universal standards (Nietzsche, Thus Spoke Zarathustra, 1883).

Existentialism and the Individual's Response: Existentialist thinkers, such as Jean-Paul Sartre and Simone de Beauvoir, emphasized the role of individual freedom and responsibility in creating personal meaning. Sartre's notion of existential freedom underscores the power and burden of crafting one's values and purpose. At the same time, de Beauvoir's existentialism expands this to encompass gender and social roles, emphasizing the significance of personal choice and responsibility (Sartre, Being and Nothingness, 1943; de Beauvoir, The Second Sex, 1949).

Evolutionary Biology and the Meaning of Life: Charles Darwin's theory of evolution and natural selection challenged traditional notions of purpose by highlighting survival and reproduction as fundamental biological imperatives. This naturalistic perspective provides insights into the biological basis of human existence and its implications for understanding meaning (Darwin, On the Origin of Species, 1859). Darwin's work encourages a reevaluation of purpose in light of evolutionary processes.

The Selfish Gene and Dawkins' Perspective: Richard Dawkins's concept of the "selfish gene" further redefines purpose by focusing on genetic imperatives and evolutionary strategies. This perspective highlights how genetic survival drives behavior and challenges traditional ideas of individual purpose, shifting the focus to the evolutionary underpinnings of human actions and motivations (Dawkins, The Selfish Gene, 1976).

The universe's indifference and the Universe's Scale: The vastness of the universe and its indifference to human existence underscore the insignificance of individual lives in the cosmic context. Scientific perspectives on cosmic scale and randomness challenge our sense of intrinsic purpose, highlighting the contrast between human concerns and the indifferent expanse of the universe (Hawking, A Brief History of Time, 1988).

Limits of Scientific Understanding: While science offers valuable insights, it also has limitations in addressing existential questions. The boundaries of scientific inquiry highlight the necessity for philosophical and personal approaches to understanding human existence. The interplay between scientific findings and existential reflections enriches our comprehension of meaning and purpose (Penrose, The Road to Reality, 2004).

Embracing the Absurd and Creating Meaning: Camus's approach to adopting the absurd and creating personal meaning underscores the possibility of finding fulfillment despite the lack of intrinsic purpose. Practical strategies for personal exploration, such as creative expression and self-reflection, offer ways to navigate the complexities of existence and cultivate individual significance (Camus, The Myth of Sisyphus, 1942).

Philosophical and Scientific Reconciliation: Integrating philosophical and scientific perspectives provides a richer understanding of existential issues, combining insights from different disciplines to offer a more comprehensive view of meaning and purpose. A multidisciplinary approach allows for a deeper exploration of human existence and the search for significance (Nagel, The View from Nowhere, 1986).

The Role of Art, Literature, and Culture: Art, literature, and culture serve as profound avenues for exploring and expressing existential questions. Through their emotional resonance and symbolic depth, creative works offer insight into the complexities of the human condition. From the haunting stillness of Edvard Munch's The Scream (1893) to the absurd dialogues in Samuel Beckett's Waiting for Godot (1953), these expressions reflect the anxiety, hope, alienation, and search for meaning that define the existential journey. In doing so, they not only mirror personal struggles but also foster collective understanding and dialogue about the human experience.

Personal Reflections and Applications: Engaging individuals in personal reflection is a powerful way to confront and navigate existential questions. Practical tools such as Viktor Frankl's logotherapy and Stephen Covey's concept of personal mission statements provide structured approaches to self-exploration. These methods empower individuals to identify core values, clarify life goals, and cultivate a deeper sense of purpose. By actively participating in this reflective process, readers can construct meaning in their lives even in the face of uncertainty and adversity (Frankl, Man's Search for Meaning, 1946; Covey, The 7 Habits of Highly Effective People, 1989).

2. INVITATION FOR READERS TO CONTINUE THEIR EXISTENTIAL EXPLORATION

As we conclude this journey through existential inquiry, it is essential to acknowledge that the exploration of meaning is a deeply personal and continuous endeavor. This book has laid out a framework for understanding the complexities of existence and offered various perspectives and tools to aid in the search for purpose. However, the journey does not end here. It is a lifelong process that invites ongoing engagement and reflection.

Embrace the Ongoing Nature of Existential Inquiry: The search for meaning is not a one-time event but a dynamic and evolving process. Readers are encouraged to view their existential exploration as a continuous journey rather than a final destination. This involves regular self-reflection, openness to new experiences, and adaptability to changing perspectives. By recognizing that existential inquiry is an ongoing process, readers can maintain a sense of curiosity and commitment to their personal quest for meaning.

Engage with Diverse Perspectives: Readers should actively seek out and engage with various philosophical, scientific, and artistic perspectives. Diverse viewpoints can offer fresh insights and deepen their understanding of existential issues. Exploring contemporary thinkers, recent scientific advancements, and innovative artistic expressions can provide new dimensions to their search for meaning. Engaging with a broad range of ideas not only enriches their perspective but also fosters a more nuanced understanding of life's complexities.

Apply Insights to Daily Life: Readers should apply the insights and strategies discussed in this book to their daily lives. Whether through creative expression, personal reflection, or philosophical inquiry, integrating these approaches into everyday experiences can help navigate existential challenges and enhance personal fulfillment. By actively applying these insights, readers can translate theoretical understanding into practical actions that resonate with their unique experiences and aspirations.

Cultivate a Community of Exploration: Readers can connect with others interested in existential questions. Joining discussion groups, attending lectures, or participating in philosophical and artistic communities can provide valuable support and inspiration. Engaging with a community of like-minded individuals offers opportunities for collaborative exploration, exchange of ideas, and mutual encouragement. A shared journey can enrich personal growth and provide meaningful connections.

Reflect and Adapt: Readers are encouraged to self-reflect and be adaptable in their existential journey regularly. The search for meaning is inherently personal and subject to change over time. Periodically reflecting on their experiences, insights, and evolving beliefs will help readers stay engaged with their quest for purpose. Being open to adapting their approaches and perspectives as they grow ensures that their exploration remains relevant and responsive to their changing needs and circumstances.

FINAL THOUGHTS: EMBRACING THE ENDLESS QUEST

Ultimately, the journey through existential inquiry reveals that meaning is neither fixed nor externally bestowed—it is something we actively create and continually redefine. This exploration challenges us to embrace uncertainty, to live courageously in the face of the absurd, and to recognize that the absence of intrinsic purpose is not a limitation but an invitation to author our own lives. As we move forward, let us carry with us the humility to accept life's mysteries, the resilience to confront its challenges, and the openness to discover meaning in unexpected places. The path of existential discovery is endless, rich with opportunities for growth, transformation, and connection. It is a profoundly human endeavor—one that transcends any single philosophy, science, or art form— inviting each of us to participate fully in the creation of a life worth living. The journey continues, and with it, the promise of new insights, deeper understanding, and the ongoing renewal of purpose.

APPENDICES

APPENDIX A: GLOSSARY OF KEY TERMS AND CONCEPTS

Absurd: A philosophical concept articulated by Albert Camus, referring to the conflict between humans' intrinsic desire for meaning and the universe's inherent indifference. The absurd emerges when individuals recognize the lack of intrinsic meaning in the universe while still striving for purpose.

Übermensch: A concept introduced by Friedrich Nietzsche, often translated as "Overman" or "Superman." It represents an individual who transcends conventional values and creates their own values and purpose in a world devoid of absolute truths.

Nihilism: A philosophical perspective, associated with Friedrich Nietzsche, characterized by the belief that life lacks intrinsic purpose or value. Nihilism arises from the "death of God" and the recognition that traditional sources of meaning are no longer viable.

The Will to Live: A concept from Arthur Schopenhauer's philosophy, referring to the fundamental driving force behind human actions and existence. It represents an intrinsic, often irrational, striving that leads to suffering and dissatisfaction.

The Selfish Gene: A term coined by Richard Dawkins in his book The Selfish Gene (Dawkins, 1976), to describe the idea that genes, rather than individuals or species, are the primary unit of selection in evolution. It suggests that the survival and replication of genes shape behaviors.

Existentialism: is a philosophical movement that emphasizes individual freedom, choice, and responsibility. Existentialists argue that individuals must create their own meaning and values in a world that does not offer intrinsic purpose.

The universe's indifference: The idea that the universe operates without regard for human concerns or aspirations. It underscores the vast scale and randomness of the cosmos, highlighting the insignificance of individual human lives in a cosmic context.

The Myth of Sisyphus: An essay by Albert Camus in which he uses the Greek mythological figure of Sisyphus, condemned to eternally roll a boulder up a hill, as a metaphor for the human condition. Camus suggests that Sisyphus as a symbol of absurdity of his situation.

Natural Selection: A key concept in Charles Darwin's theory of evolution suggests that organisms that are better adapted to their environment are more likely to survive and reproduce. Natural selection drives the evolution of species and impacts the search for meaning by focusing on survival and reproduction.

Existential Angst: The deep anxiety or dread experienced when individuals confront the inherent meaninglessness of existence and the freedom to create their own meaning.

APPENDIX B: RECOMMENDED READING AND RESOURCE BOOKS

1. Camus, Albert. The Myth of Sisyphus. Gallimard, 1942.
   - A foundational text in existentialism, exploring absurdism and how individuals can find meaning despite it.
2. Schopenhauer, Arthur. The World as Will and Representation. E.P. Dutton, 1818.
   - Schopenhauer's seminal work discussing the concept of the Will and its implications for human suffering and existence.
3. Nietzsche, Friedrich. Thus Spoke Zarathustra. Penguin Classics, 1883.
   - Nietzsche's exploration of the Übermensch and his critique of traditional values and nihilism.
4. Sartre, Jean-Paul. Being and Nothingness. Washington Square Press, 1943.
   - Sartre's comprehensive work on existentialism, freedom, and the nature of existence.
5. Dawkins, Richard. The Selfish Gene. Oxford University Press, 1976.
   - Dawkins's influential book on evolutionary biology and the role of genes in shaping behavior and understanding of purpose.
6. Darwin, Charles. On the Origin of Species. John Murray, 1859.
   - Darwin's groundbreaking work on natural selection and its impact on the understanding of life's purpose.

7. Nagel, Thomas. The View from Nowhere. Oxford University Press, 1986.
   o An exploration of the limits of scientific understanding and philosophical perspectives on meaning and objectivity.
8. Kabat-Zinn, Jon. Wherever You Go, There You Are: Mindfulness Meditation in Everyday Life. Hyperion, 1994.
   o A guide to mindfulness and meditation practices for personal reflection and existential exploration.
9. Frankl, Viktor E. Man's Search for Meaning. Beacon Press, 1946.
   o Frankl's account of his experiences in a concentration camp and his psychological approach to finding meaning in suffering.
10. Sennett, Richard. The Craftsman. Yale University Press, 2008.
    o A study of craftsmanship and its relationship to personal meaning and fulfillment.

ARTICLES AND ESSAYS

1. Beckett, Samuel. Waiting for Godot. Grove Press, 1953.
   o A seminal play that explores themes of existentialism and the search for meaning through absurdist drama.

2. **Munch, Edvard. The Scream. 1893.**
   o An iconic painting reflecting existential angst and the human condition.

ONLINE RESOURCES

1. **Stanford Encyclopedia of Philosophy:** Articles on existentialism, nihilism, and other philosophical concepts.
2. **Internet Encyclopedia of Philosophy:** Detailed entries on various existential and philosophical topics.
3. **Coursera and edX:** Online courses on existential philosophy and related subjects.

DOCUMENTARIES AND LECTURES

1. **The Examined Life (2008):** A documentary directed by Astra Taylor, featuring contemporary philosophers such as Cornel West, Judith Butler, and Peter Singer, each sharing insights on the search for meaning.
2. **The Pervert's Guide to Ideology (2012):** A documentary directed by Sophie Fiennes, featuring philosopher Slavoj Žižek as he analyzes film clips to explore how ideology shapes our everyday beliefs and existential outlook.

APPENDIX C: INDEX

BIBLIOGRAPHY

1. Allen, W. (Director). (1977). Annie Hall [Film]. United Artists.
2. Aristotle. (350 B.C.E./2009). Nicomachean ethics (W. D. Ross, Trans.; J. A. Smith, Ed.). Oxford University Press.
3. Armstrong, K. (2009). The case for God. Knopf.
4. Bandura, A. (2006). Agentic perspective. In G. W. Bowers & M. J. H. S. Masters (Eds.), The self and society in changing times (pp. 167–189). Cambridge University Press.
5. Baumeister, R. F., & Leary, M. R. (1995). The need to belong: Desire for interpersonal attachments as a fundamental human motivation. Psychological Bulletin, 117(3), 497–529.
6. Beckett, S. (1953). Waiting for Godot. London: Faber and Faber.
7. Bostrom, N. (2014). Superintelligence: Paths, dangers, strategies. Oxford University Press.
8. Camus, A. (1956). The fall. Alfred A. Knopf.
9. Camus, A. (1991). The myth of Sisyphus (J. O'Brien, Trans.). Vintage Books. (Original work published 1942)
10. Camus, A. (1991). The plague (S. Gilbert, Trans.). Vintage Books. (Original work published 1947)
11. Covey, S. R. (1989). The 7 habits of highly effective people: Powerful lessons in personal change. Free Press.
12. Csikszentmihalyi, M. (1990). Flow: The psychology of optimal experience. Harper & Row.
13. Darwin, C. (1859). On the origin of species by means of natural selection. John Murray.
14. Dawkins, R. (1982). The long reach of the gene. Oxford University Press.
15. Dawkins, R. (1976). The selfish gene. Oxford University Press.
16. de Beauvoir, S. (1949). The second sex (C. Borde & S. Malovany-Chevallier, Trans.). Vintage Books.

17. Dennett, D. C. (1995). Darwin's dangerous idea: Evolution and the meanings of life. Simon & Schuster.

18. Dewey, J. (1927). The public and its problems. Swallow Press.

19. Durkheim, É. (1912). The elementary forms of religious life. Alcan.

20. Eagleman, D. (2011). Incognito: The secret lives of the brain. Pantheon Books.

21. Foucault, M. (1975). Discipline and punish: The birth of the prison (A. Sheridan, Trans.). Pantheon Books.

22. Frankl, V. E. (1946). Man's search for meaning. Beacon Press.

23. Gould, S. J. (2002). The structure of evolutionary theory. Belknap Press of Harvard University Press.

24. Hawking, S. (1988). A brief history of time: From the Big Bang to black holes. Bantam Books.

25. Hawking, S. (2010). The grand design. Bantam Books.

26. Harman, G. (1996). Moral relativism and moral objectivity. Blackwell Publishing.

27. Heidegger, M. (1927). Being and time (J. Macquarrie & E. Robinson, Trans.). Harper & Row.

28. Hughes, L. (1940). The big sea. Knopf.

29. Hurston, Z. N. (1937). Their eyes were watching God. J. B. Lippincott & Co.

30. Kant, I. (1785). Groundwork of the metaphysics of morals (H. J. Paton, Trans.). Hutchinson.

31. Kabat-Zinn, J. (1994). Wherever you go, there you are: Mindfulness meditation in everyday life. Hyperion.

32. Kafka, F. (1998). The metamorphosis (D. Wyllie, Trans.). Schocken Books. (Original work published 1915)

33. Kurzweil, R. (2005). The singularity is near: When humans transcend biology. Viking.

34. Lyotard, J.-F. (1979). The postmodern condition: A report on knowledge (G. Bennington & B. Massumi, Trans.). University of Minnesota Press.

35. Malchiodi, C. (2006). The art therapy sourcebook. McGraw-Hill.

36. Maslow, A. H. (1954). Motivation and personality. Harper & Row.

37. Nagel, T. (1971). The absurd. The Journal of Philosophy, 68(20), 716–727.

38. Nagel, T. (1997). The last word. Oxford University Press.

39. Nagel, T. (1986). The view from nowhere. Oxford University Press.

40. Norton, J. (2009). The vision board: The secret to an extraordinary life. Atria Books.

41. Pennebaker, J. W. (1997). Opening up: The healing power of expressing emotions. Guilford Press.

42. Pinker, S. (2011). The better angels of our nature: Why violence has declined. Viking.

43. Pinker, S. (2002). The blank slate: The modern denial of human nature. Viking.

44. Popper, K. R. (1959). The logic of scientific discovery. Routledge.

45. Roszak, T. (1992). The voice of the earth: An exploration of ecopsychology. Simon & Schuster.

46. Sagan, C. (1994). Pale blue dot: A vision of the human future in space. Random House.

47. Sandel, M. J. (2007). The case against perfection: Ethics in the age of genetic engineering. Harvard University Press.

48. Schopenhauer, A. (1840). On the basis of morality (C. Schlegel, Trans.). Lonergan.

49. Schopenhauer, A. (1818). The world as will and representation (E. F. J. Payne, Trans.; Vols. 1–2). Dover Publications.

50. Sartre, J.-P. (1943). Being and nothingness (H. E. Barnes, Trans.). Washington Square Press.

51. Sartre, J.-P. (1946). Existentialism is a humanism (C. Macomber, Trans.). Yale University Press.

52. Sartre, J.-P. (2007). Nausea (L. Alexander, Trans.). New Directions Publishing. (Original work published 1938)

53. Sennett, R. (2008). The craftsman. Yale University Press.

54. Seligman, M. E. P. (2002). Authentic happiness: Using the new positive psychology to realize your potential for lasting fulfillment. Free Press.

55. Seligman, M. E. P. (2011). Flourish: A visionary new understanding of happiness and well-being. Atria Books.

56. Suzuki, S. (1970). Zen mind, beginner's mind. Weatherhill.
57. Turkle, S. (2011). Alone together: Why we expect more from technology and less from each other. Basic Books.
58. Watts, A. W. (1957). The way of Zen. Pantheon Books.
59. Wilson, E. O. (1998). Consilience: The unity of knowledge. Alfred A. Knopf.
60. Wilson, E. O. (2012). The social conquest of Earth. Harvard University Press.
61. Young, I. M. (1990). Justice and the politics of difference. Princeton University Press.
62. Yalom, I. D. (1980). Existential psychotherapy. Basic Books.

ENDNOTES

1. Camus, A. (1942). The myth of Sisyphus. Gallimard.
2. Camus explores the idea that the universe is indifferent to human struggles. The "benign indifference" refers to the universe's lack of concern for human existence, which can be both a source of despair and a liberating realization that prompts individuals to find their own meaning in an otherwise indifferent world.
3. Schopenhauer, A. (1818). The world as will and representation (E. F. J. Payne, Trans.). Dover Publications.
4. Schopenhauer's philosophy posits that human suffering is a fundamental aspect of existence due to the insatiable nature of human desires. His pessimistic view is rooted in the belief that life is driven by an irrational and ceaseless will, leading to perpetual dissatisfaction.
5. Nietzsche, F. (1883–1885). Thus spoke Zarathustra (G. Parkes, Trans.). Oxford University Press.
6. Nietzsche challenges traditional values and proposes the concept of the Übermensch, or "Overman," who creates his own values and meaning in a world devoid of intrinsic purpose. The Übermensch represents an ideal of self-overcoming and creative power in the face of an indifferent universe.
7. Darwin, C. (1859). On the origin of species. John Murray.
8. Darwin's theory of evolution by natural selection provides a scientific framework for understanding the development of life on Earth. The idea that life evolves through random mutations and natural selection challenges traditional notions of purposeful design and implies that life's complexity arises from natural processes.

9. Dawkins, R. (1976). The selfish gene. Oxford University Press.
10. Dawkins argues that genes, rather than individuals or species, are the primary units of selection. His theory emphasizes that the apparent design and complexity of life can be explained by the evolutionary success of genes acting in their own interest, which further challenges the idea of a purposeful universe.
11. Integration of philosophy and science.
12. The integration of philosophical and scientific perspectives in this book highlights the multifaceted nature of existential inquiry. By examining existential questions through both philosophical discourse and scientific understanding, this approach provides a comprehensive framework for exploring the meaning of life in an apparently indifferent universe.

These endnotes provide additional context and sources for the philosophical and scientific discussions presented in the book, offering readers a deeper understanding of the key concepts and theories explored.

www.ingramcontent.com/pod-product-compliance
Lightning Source LLC
LaVergne TN
LVHW020010190725
816534LV00011B/187